When I

Dances

JUDITH HOOD

Judith Hood Publishing

Maldon,

Essex,

England.

www.judithhood.co.uk

ISBN   978-1-8381741-0-1 (Paperback edition)

ISBN   978-1-8381741-1-8 (Digital edition)

Cover picture illustrated by Ujala Shahid.

Cover designed by Nick Constantinou and Michael Burl

Printed in Great Britain by Biddles Books Limited, King's Lynn, Norfolk

It is never too late

And you are never too old !

Shaun & Michelle

Much Love

Judith
xx

Despair

The food poisoning symptoms lasted a week and I really do not know how I wasn't hospitalised, I have never felt so ill. Mum has popped in to see me each day and Paul has done a wonderful job of looking after me. But now it is the middle of the second week and to be honest it is simply easier to just lie here. Only Paul knows about the screaming woman. She has occupied my mind for some considerable time now. It isn't constant, in fact since I have been ill she has been a little quieter, probably because she has not been quite so troubled whilst I lie here hidden from the world. The feeling of falling into the abyss has also lessened which is a great relief as that is almost unbearable, it is like nothing I have ever experienced before but then mentally I have never been in such a dreadful state before. The only way I can describe the feeling is that I will be going about a simple daily task and suddenly all my worries flood my mind and it is as if the world drops away and I am falling, as I fall there is nothing to hold onto or grab and all that is below me is the abyss.

Being so ill has given me the wonderful gift of not being able to think. In the past I have found it so frustrating how much the mind dulls when I have a bad cold or a Migraine etc. No one wants to be unwell and usually I fight to rid myself of whatever ails me as fast as I can to jump back into the hustle and bustle of life but today I find myself contemplating the fact that it seems so much easier to just lie here. Having said all of that, the very fact that I am thinking this shows that I cannot hide here much longer. My mind is getting sharper every day and the thought of getting out of bed and allowing the screaming woman back in is almost too much to bear. Paul has been so patient, he knows how low I have become and I know that he simply does not know what he can do to help. Frankly I don't think anyone can. I got myself here and I just do not know what to do.

Suddenly Brian enters the room. He is standing by the bed and telling me to not be frightened. It never ceases to amaze me, how tall he is, he is such a huge presence, he seems to glow and shimmer which is wonderful to see. He says he is going to lift me up. Somehow this does not seem strange and I allow him to do so. I am lying on my side and he scoops me up almost as you would a toddler. As he picks me up I realise that I need to put my arm across my chest and into his chest or it will simply flop backwards. As I do this I glance down and I see myself on the bed putting my arm up across my chest...... At that moment I realise I am out of body.....

2

3 Years Earlier

January 2007

It is late but that does not stop me from changing into my PJ's and sitting down at my computer for a quick look at my e mails. Tonight's date had been an eye opener. We met at a local pub and spent the entire evening talking about ourselves and it became very clear that we had absolutely nothing in common to the extent that if he said black the chances were I would say white. He loved spending a two week holiday by the pool and I could think of nothing worse as I find it hard to sit still for more than two minutes. When I mentioned long rambles through the countryside he looked so appalled that I thought he was going to make a run for it there and then. And so it went on, whatever I loved, he hated and vice versa. So we had a laugh and finished the evening by agreeing in a very comical way never to cross paths again.

Although it had been amusing it also leaves me feeling a little lost. After my marriage broke down I spent some time alone but realised quite quickly that I was lonely. Thirty years together with my ex-husband had found me institutionalised and I wanted to be with someone but that was proving easier said than done. At 46 one could not exactly go clubbing and I really did not know how else I was going to find someone to love. So after much deliberation I had decided to try internet dating.

Poor Mandy, one of my closest friends from Blue Falcons has to spend many a long hour listening to me complaining about the trials and tribulations of internet dating. She has been such a support since I split from my husband as have many of my friends.

You would think that I would have discovered that tonight's date and I had nothing in common after chatting online before meeting but I have realised after many months of dating that it is simpler to meet quickly. I have "fallen" for a couple of men after weeks and weeks of exchanging e mails only to find that on meeting, there simply is no spark, not for any particular reason but if it is not there, it is not something that can be forced. It sounds daft to suggest that you can fall for someone just from exchanging e mails but do not forget that internet dating leaves a person feeling very vulnerable and you would not be doing it unless you were lonely so it is very easy to start developing feelings for someone via e mail, especially if they are saying all the right things. Having said that, I am now going to contradict myself. I did meet a chap very early on in the process who was not my type at all. In fact at that point I had not joined a dating site, I met him in a chat room which my mate had suggested when she heard how lonely I was feeling. This man began chatting and I

4

told him I was not looking to date but he was persistent, I give him that, and eventually after a couple of weeks of chatting we agreed to meet. I have a friend, Jo, who was also on a dating site and I gave her the details of where we were meeting and promised to keep her posted. So James and I met up and had a lovely evening which mainly consisted of us joking about the fact that I still had no intention of dating.

We met on several occasions for drinks "as friends" but very soon I started to fall for him and then suffered the bombshell of discovering he was Married. I was devastated. I am extremely honest and trustworthy and would never knowingly become the other woman. So very sadly I said goodbye and we went our separate ways with me building my first little wall against being hurt like that again.

Bear in mind, my former husband had pretty much been my only boyfriend and we met when I was 17 so mentally I think I was like an 18 year old when it came to the dating game. I have been dating for about a year now and during that time I have learnt a lot of lessons, many of them not good. It is a source of considerable amusement for Jo and I; the weird and wonderful men out there but to be fair I have it on good authority that there are a fair number of weird women too. Jo and I always exchange details of where we were going and who we were meeting to give a little security to our dates.

One of the dangers of Internet dating is how quickly you can become obsessed with someone, I am aware of this and yet somehow it seems impossible to stop it from happening. Some time ago I messaged a man whose face really appealed to me. His profile did not say much at all but I thought it was worth an e mail. He responded straight away with just one line. I then sent him a long message rather taking the mickey out of the fact that he had only written one line. He then sent a slightly longer message reacting to what I had said but it was still relatively short. That was enough to peak my interest and I sent yet another comical e mail back to him. His reply was much longer this time and written very much in the same vein as my own.

And so we were off, e mailing daily but no verbal phone contact. After about a week he messaged to ask if we could meet. I said I would and we exchanged numbers. As I was getting ready for the date which really for me does not take too long, a shower and drying my hair is about it really as I am not one for make-up, my phone rang. It was him. He said he needed to talk to me about something before we met. He went on to explain that he had a mate who used internet dating sites to find women who he would then meet but he was simply out to have sex and was not looking for a relationship. His method was to just message women or reply to women who messaged him and gradually work his way through them. He told me that this friend had gone on holiday and would not have internet access whilst he was away and had

6

asked his friend (the man I was speaking to) to keep the women he was presently messaging "on the boil". This was why his first two messages were so brief, he was keeping in touch without getting any deeper. However he claimed that my message had amused him so much he could not resist answering and then my second message had the same effect and he began talking to me. However I, of course, believed I was talking to the man I had originally messaged and whose picture I had seen.

I was absolutely devastated. I could not get past the fact that he had lied. I am an extremely honest person and cannot bear lying. He told me that once he got talking to me he really started to like me and was single himself but did not know how to tell me I was not talking to who I thought I was. I could understand this and had he been honest with me almost immediately I might have been able to understand but it had been too long. I do not consider myself to be so shallow that looks are all that matters. I would have been happy to meet him as we had had some really good conversations via e mail but it was too late, the damage was done. I was so hurt, I simply could not go and meet him. To me trust is vitally important in a relationship and he had lost my trust before we had even met. As you can imagine following this incident, my nerves are always a little on edge when getting to know someone new.

One man took me on a date and we got on quite well and he asked if he could take me to dinner, I agreed and he told me he would call me. He did call me a couple of days later to tell me he had had a date with a woman who 'took his breath away!' This hurt me on a number of levels.... I would have liked to think I took his breath away, clearly not.... I also was a little taken aback that he had had a date with another woman almost immediately after meeting me. I now realise that I was being a little old fashioned with that attitude, if I was talking to someone online I only spoke to that one person. I am extremely faithful and almost felt it was wrong to talk to more than one person at a time. I did not change that attitude and it did hurt when I realised men and I am sure many women, did not take the same route. As you will begin to realise I am a little naïve, not at all familiar with the workings of the world, I had lived in a little bubble bringing up my three boys in a village and stepping out of that bubble was proving to be a little shocking for me.

Anyway back to the man whose breath I *did not* take away. He called me a couple of months later by which time I had been seeing a man for a few weeks. I answered the phone, he said who he was and then asked what I wanted from a relationship. He asked if I wanted a bit of fun or was I looking for a full on relationship? I told him frankly that although Marriage was certainly not my first intention I was looking to have a relationship with someone and I was not simply out for 'a bit of fun' as he so bluntly put it. He then went on to explain that the amazingly gorgeous woman that he had found was 'crazy' and all she was interested in was marrying him and he felt she was after his money. I did not even bother to enlighten him to the fact that money and things have never been an interest of mine and that a happy and healthy life are far more important. I simply told him thanks but no thanks and that I was now seeing someone. Snooze you lose! I did not say the last bit of course as I do have a little decorum.

So here I am, another date bites the dust and I am feeling a little low. As mentioned earlier I did see a couple of men for a few weeks at a time but baggage is a terrible thing sometimes and can destroy a relationship before it even gets off the ground.

Is it time to throw in the towel with this internet dating? I really would like to meet someone and I do not know how else to do it. I have a friend who could not bear the thought of trawling through dating websites and she has chosen to join a dinner club where the group you meet have been put together by an agency who has attempted to match like-minded people and they meet regularly for dinner. By doing this hopefully some will find a partner by becoming friends first. It is a nice idea but I have a slight phobia of eating in front of people, convinced I am going to end up with food all over my chest and face. There are no grounds for this fear as I really am capable of eating like an adult but we cannot help our phobias and so here I am sitting at a computer staring at yet more faces of prospective dates. Time for bed I think.

One Last Try

One could never accuse me of giving up. If nothing else I have a grim determination once I set my mind to something.

It is mid-afternoon and I have spent the day catching up on paperwork in my office which is a very small room in our house but it does the job and really, it is where I go to escape from the world. I am slowly winding down my small business, it is a recruitment agency for people wishing to do part time office work. I employ them and find the work for them and sometimes I will fill a job myself to bring in extra money. It has given me an income throughout the boy's childhoods but now I confess I just do not want to do it anymore. With my marriage over and my sons needing me less and less, life seems to be taking many new routes. I do not know where it is taking me but I have learnt to trust I will find my way.

The boys are all out. I have caught up on the housework so now I have decided to have a little look at my messages on the dating site. I have to say it is a little like a drug, I want to give up but just want one last little look. No new messages, what a surprise! I do find that I have to make the first move which is a little soul-destroying in itself. Although occasionally a man will approach me, I had one recently he must have been 80 at least, he had a picture of himself standing proudly in his kilt. He messaged me to say that I looked very nice and he would be willing to move from Scotland to Essex to be with me! Honestly, you could not make it up. He had not even spoken to me and was suggesting moving countries for me! I read it with an air of despair, is this really what I am reduced to?

As I am staring despondently at my empty message box pictures are flashing up at the side of the screen showing men who are presently online. A face appears and my heart does a little leap as he looks lovely. You would think by now that I would have learnt my lesson. A year of sending messages to men who I find attractive and who pretty much never reply should have been enough of a hint that I am aiming too high. But one last little peep at this one's profile cannot do any harm surely.

I click on his picture which takes me straight to his profile and as I start to read the hairs on my arms and on the back of my neck begin to stand. His entire profile is dedicated to talking about his ghost investigation group. Well if nothing else it seems we have something in common. My entire life has been one strange occurrence after another, so much so that at one place I worked they called me 'spooky Jude'.

It is a sign, surely. There I was about to give up and this lovely looking man is interested in ghosts. Please don't think me shallow, I absolutely appreciate that looks are not everything but they are a start and there is something about this man's face that I simply cannot resist. I am going to go for it and message him…. I will tell him one of my stories, what harm could it do?

As I am no stranger to the weird and wonderful I have a huge array of stories to choose from so which shall I send him? I do not want to frighten him off before we even get started so I think I shall keep it light. Ok, here we go!

Hi, my name is Judith, I just read your profile and thought I would tell you one of my tales, I will be interested to hear what you think.

The first time I recall seeing a ghost I was about 14. My Mum and I were in the kitchen, my Dad had taken my three siblings out somewhere and I was rather enjoying having Mum to myself for a change. I was leaning against the wall of an arch that led from the kitchen into the dining room. The house is open plan and you can walk in a full circle from the dining room, through the kitchen, round through the lounge and back to the dining room. As I was chatting, the top of my head became really cold, almost as if someone had placed an ice pack on my head. The cold feeling started to travel down my body and as it did, it warmed up again above it, so it was almost like a slice of cold travelling down my body. As this was

13

happening, out of the corner of my eye I saw someone walk through the kitchen. They came from behind me and walked through the kitchen and round into the lounge. Now bearing in mind, I was chatting, I was aware of the strange coldness that was travelling down my body and therefore the person walking through the kitchen was the last thing on my mind. Once the cold had reached my feet and then disappeared and I could focus again, I asked my Mum who was in the house. She assured me that we were the only ones at home. Well I knew what I had seen so I went off to find whoever it was and searched the house from top to bottom. No one was there. I became a little distressed as I could not understand what was happening.

Mum took me through to the lounge and sat me down and explained to me that when she was a child, at the age of three, her Father had passed away. He had been very ill but Mum was also ill in another hospital and her Father, against medical advice had left hospital in order to visit my Mum. It seems this was too much for him and he died soon after visiting her

Mum was brought up in a pub, The Black Horse, on the Mile End Road in the East End of London. After my biological Grandad's death my Nana continued to run the pub on her own and eventually married one of the regulars; this was the man I knew to be my Grandad. Nana and Grandad had the pub during the war years and right up until the 1970's. Mum has a Sister by her natural Dad and then when Nana re-married they went on to have four more daughters. Unfortunately one of the girls, Shirley, died in an accident at the pub when she was only three years old. Brenda the youngest of the girls had an invisible friend for years. She called her Jean Oddhams and the family even had to go so far as to set a place at the dinner table for Jean. To this day and with what I now know, I firmly believe that Jean Oddhams was the spirit of Shirley.

Before Shirley's death people had started to notice strange occurrences in the pub and these continued right up until Nana and Grandad left the pub. Almost simultaneously with them leaving my Mum started to notice strange goings on in our house. She decided eventually that her Dad had come to stay with us rather than move on with my Nana.

As soon as Mum had finished this tale, all became clear. I had seen the ghost of my Grandad. Now you might think that this would worry a 14 year old child, but not at all, I was perfectly comfortable with the idea of a spirit living in our house. We called him 'him' and if anything mysterious occurred Mum would just say to me "it must be him".

Phew that was longer than I intended, I hope it did not bore you too much.

Message sent. Was it too long? Should I have said I hope it did not bore you? That is putting ideas in his head. I do wish I didn't immediately start second guessing myself the minute I have spoken. Unfortunately this is precisely the effect internet dating has on you. Constantly questioning everything you do and say, overthinking to the maximum. My boys are always telling me I overthink. Is this me overthinking about overthinking?

Oh my goodness!!! He has replied. My hand is actually shaking on the mouse. I hope he has not just told me to clear off. I could of course read the message and put myself out of my misery. Ok Judith, deep breath aaaand open!

Hi. Great story, I have never heard of the ice cold feeling travelling down the body before. It is really interesting, it was almost as if you felt him as he passed you! I am very aware of cold spots in a room or feeling a cold area against your body if a spirit is near but never travelling down the body before.

He liked it. Relief swamps my body and I excitedly read on.

It sounds as though your Nana and Grandad had a very interesting life, I cannot imagine running a pub through the war years and beyond. So did they stay in the East End of London throughout the Blitz?

Have I died and gone to heaven? Not only did he like the story, he is showing interest in my family. Ok Jude, get a grip, this is one message, possibly just being polite. Be still my beating heart.

Yes they did stay in London. The girls were evacuated, they were split up which was sad, I do not think my Mum had a very good time whilst she was away, she does not really talk about it. Nana told me tales of having to go down to the underground tube stations during the raids or they would go into the cellar of their pub which was kitted out for hiding in during the bombing. The pub survived the bombing which was a godsend as it was how they made their living. Of course we all know that many were not so lucky. Have you always lived in Cambridge?

Have you always lived in Cambridge? What sort of inane question was that? But I really was not sure where to go from there. God I hate this, maybe I should just give up and live out my life as a spinster, a mad cat woman. But I could not even get that right as I am not overly keen on cats.

Yes, born and bred in Cambridge. What about you, where do you live?

Uh oh. Do I tell him where I live? He could be a mad axe murderer for all I know. Ok give a rough area: that will be safe enough for the moment.

I live in Chelmsford, Essex. In a village just outside the town. What do you do for a living?

That wasn't too nosy was it? This is the other problem with e mailing, you have time in between whilst waiting, hoping for a reply, to consider and doubt the intelligence of what you have just said.

> *I am a Security Officer at the Anglia Ruskin University in Cambridge. I have finished my shift and I am using one of the public computers to speak to you but I am afraid I have to go and pick up my Son. Could I have your number I would really like to give you a call this evening?*

Oh flip, is this the brush off? The excuse to get rid of me? Well if it is no harm in giving him my number because he is probably going to completely ignore it. So I give it to him and ask if he could call me after 8.30pm by which time the boys will either be out or hidden in their bedrooms on their computer games. He tells me that is fine and that he will speak to me later.

Off I go then, back to the real world. Dinner to prepare, three hungry young men to feed. I refer to them as boys but actually they are 16, 19 and 21. As I head for the kitchen I wonder; will he call? I doubt it but a little bit of me is very excited.

That Voice

He called!! I had taken myself off to my bedroom at 8.00pm so as not to be disturbed and at exactly 8.30pm my phone rang. I knew I had to play it calm, not let him think I was desperate. So I took the light-hearted route. He said hello and every bit of me melted, he had the most gorgeous voice. We ended up talking for two hours and the strange thing was it did not seem like that length of time at all. A lot of it was silliness which frankly was probably just what I needed. I cannot remember laughing that much for what seems like years. I feel like my Nana when I say "it was a real tonic". I went to sleep feeling like I was floating on air.

He has promised to call back again this evening. He works shifts, four on and four off and today he is off and said he could call anytime but I asked if we could make it the same sort of time in the evening then I know I will not be disturbed.

I cannot stop smiling. We talked for some time about his love of the paranormal. He is so interesting and it was very refreshing to be able to talk about such things to someone who is of the same mind-set as myself. I told him that I do not believe in coincidence, I honestly believe that everything happens for a reason and that a coincidence is generally a sign of some description. He totally agreed and then explained Synchronicity to me which was fascinating. Apparently it is when a set of incidents occur which eventually lead to an outcome to which they were leading you, but this can be conceived as a huge coincidence.

So now it is 7.00pm, the day has passed in a bit of a blur really, I think I have spent a lot of it daydreaming about Paul, did I tell you that was his name? He tells me he is quite tall and has two Sons who are roughly the same age as my younger two. He is presently living with his older Son in a village on the outskirts of Cambridge. They set up home together when he separated from his long term partner.

Once again I take myself off to my bedroom to read whilst I wait for Paul's phone call. Nerves are setting in. Will he call again? Did I put him off last night?

Bang on 8.30pm my phone rings. I am overcome with relief, I feel so daft feeling like this after one phone call but I think that demonstrates my vulnerability after being let down so many times. As soon as I hear his voice my heart starts to beat so much faster. He sounds so lovely.

Once again we chat for a couple of hours. This time we are a little more sensible with each other, talking more about our past lives and how we have reached this point. He seems so understanding and I wonder if I have said too much about how sad I am being alone, he has told me he thinks I need a big hug. By the end of the call he has asked me if I would like to meet for lunch on Sunday. We chatted about where best to meet and we decided on the village of Thaxted which is between Chelmsford and Cambridge.

The next few days are busy but we find time to speak on the phone each day and before I know it Sunday arrives, it is a beautiful January day, bright sunshine but a nasty nip in the wind. We have agreed to meet in the High Street. I arrive much too early and I sit in my car, nerves making my tummy almost ache. The time we agreed is approaching so I get out of the car and go to my boot to get my jacket. Just as I am leaning into my boot a car hoots, I turn and it is him, grinning away like a Cheshire cat as he passes me looking for a space to park.

Locking up the car I begin to head in the direction he went, suddenly I see him get out of his car, he locks it and turns towards me, my legs turn to jelly. His picture did not do him justice. He is gorgeous! This may sound ridiculous but the thing that strikes me, out of everything that could have been my immediate reaction, is that he is wearing a bandana tied around his neck and a long black leather jacket. I have always felt a strange pull towards all things hippy (for want of a better word). I have seen people in the street who may be dressed differently to what would be considered the norm and I have wished I could be more like that and therefore seeing him wearing this bandana pleased me more than you would imagine.

His lopsided grin draws me to him and as I get closer, with his hands in his jacket pockets he opens the jacket. I walk up to him and putting my arms inside the jacket and around his back I lean into his chest. He wraps his arms and the jacket around me and that is how we stand for quite a few minutes, not speaking, just standing there with me tucked inside his jacket.

It would seem impossible to many I am sure but at that moment I knew; we had found each other. Something shifted within me, I felt safe and right and I could not have been happier. Thaxted is a beautiful town and the history of it dates back to before the Domesday Book, at the heart of the town is a massive church and we headed towards this. We spent a couple of hours just wandering and chatting, we sat by the windmill and shared more of our stories and then we went for lunch. We ended up spending the whole day together and by the time I came to head home I really did not want to leave him. We had arranged our next meeting and I simply could not wait.

The saying that you need to walk a mile in a person's shoes before you can comment on their actions is so true. I am sure in the past if I had heard someone declaring their love for a person within a very short time of meeting them I would be very doubtful of their ability to know how they really feel. Perhaps apart from anything else, our age had something to do with it. You do get to know yourself and your likes and dislikes. I knew what I wanted from life and Paul ticked all the boxes and I knew he felt the same about me.

And so it began, travelling back and forth between Cambridge and Chelmsford. I met his two boys and he met my three. Gradually we got to know each other's families and life was good.

Discovery

During the first few months of our relationship one of the things we spent a lot of time discussing was the afterlife. Paul had loved his time with the ghost investigation group in Cambridge and had lots of interesting tales to tell. Equally he enjoyed hearing my stories from over the years; so many spooky happenings. One day whilst snuggled up together he suggested that I might be a psychic medium. He told me that after hearing so many of my tales it must be the case. I was stunned to put it mildly. I have been to see a few mediums in my time and never would I ever had imagined that I could be similar to them. One or two of these mediums had told me that I was a healer but to be honest I had always just ignored that idea.

I know that I am a confident person; I have always been one to push myself forward in all aspects of my life but this was a different thing altogether. I have always believed in 'natural leaders' maybe being the oldest child also helps but it has always come naturally to me to take the lead in most situations. I think the answer is that confidence is different to ego. I am confident in my abilities to do things but I do not have very strong self-belief.   To me a medium is someone to be admired, someone who has an amazing gift.   To consider that I was such a person, would to me, almost seem big headed.   I have difficulty explaining exactly what I mean by this but suffice to say I did not feel I was special enough to have such a gift.

Not put off by my assurances that this could not be true Paul asked me to try to contact his Mother who had died some years before and whom I had never met. I told him I had no idea how to even begin to try such a thing. He told me to clear my mind which in itself was quite a request as I have such a busy mind, it goes ten to the dozen always thinking about many things at once.

"Just take yourself to a quiet place, calm your mind and see what happens."   He smiled and nodded gently. "You can do this" he whispered. "You just have to believe in yourself."

I closed my eyes and tried to stop my thoughts from drifting. Suddenly in my minds' eye I saw what looked like an old black and white photograph of a shop. Keeping my eyes closed I began to describe to Paul what I was seeing.

"I can see a shop, like an old fashioned Haberdashery."

"OK, that makes sense, we had a shop like that just down the road from our house."

"Now I can see knitting needles and knitwear."

Paul laughed gently, "Well done! Mum used to knit stuff and the woman in the shop used to sell it for her."

"I can see a house, really clearly but it is a bit odd because there are car parts all over the front lawn."

At this Paul laughed out loud. "They are not car parts, they are motorbike parts. I dismantled a motorbike on the front lawn and my Mum was furious."

I opened my eyes and looked at him, his beautiful brown eyes were looking at me adoringly.

"That was brilliant Jude, for a first attempt to get that much information is astounding." I have to be honest here and admit that I did not 100 per cent believe what he had said. I knew how much he loved me and thought that maybe he was trying to boost me up.

The following week I went to Cambridge to visit.

"Would you like to go to the estate where I grew up and see the houses?" Paul asked me as we were sitting having a drink.

"Well that would be interesting, I would love to."

As we approached the estate Paul explained that the house that he had lived in had now been demolished but as it was a council estate there were identical houses still standing. As he pulled up in front of one of the houses I stared in disbelief, there in front of me was exactly the house I had seen in my mind; the house which had had the bike parts on the lawn. Goosebumps crept all over my body. 'How could this be possible?' Thoughts were running through my mind faster than I could process them. Question upon question entered my mind.

I turned and looked at Paul, he was grinning with excitement. He could see my dismay and was delighted by it.

"I told you. You contacted my Mum and she gave you some of her memories."

We talked and talked, for all the good it did that afternoon because I could not take it all in. I had experienced enough over the years to totally believe in the afterlife and signs etc. I fully believed in the abilities of mediums but even though I knew an awful lot of weird stuff had happened to me, the thought that I might actually be capable of contacting the Spirit World was more than I could take in.

Denise

When my boys started secondary school they joined a Gymnastic Display Team called the Blue Falcons. As you would expect I very quickly joined the adult support team and we had a wonderful time training a couple of times a week and then travelling around most weekends during the summer months doing displays at School fetes and similar type events. We were sponsored by the Royal Navy and had some wonderful visits to Portsmouth and Chatham Navy bases where we not only did displays but were treated to special insights of life on a Royal Navy base.

Naturally the adult support team became very good friends and I was frequently found telling anyone who would listen about my latest 'spooky' occurrence. Although I knew Jo originally from our village school, our children had all moved up to the same secondary school and all joined the Blue Falcons and this was where our friendship really blossomed. Of course I could not wait to tell everyone what had happened with Paul and his Mum and our visit to the house. This resulted in one of my friends asking if I would go to her house to try and do a 'Reading' for her.

It was so strange the way I had just leapt into this. To agree to go to Denise's house was a step I never imagined I would take but here we were about to attempt to contact her Dad. Paul and Denise were sitting opposite me and I closed my eyes and tried to calm myself. Paul said something but I did not hear it clearly. I opened my eyes and asked him what he had said.

"I didn't speak" said Paul, who looked confused and turned to Denise who shrugged and looked puzzled. I closed my eyes again and sure enough I heard a man's voice. A shiver ran through me and goose pimples began to raise all over my body. My eyes filled with tears and I struggled to stay calm. His voice was deep, gentle and reassuring. I spoke aloud to Denise and Paul, repeating what the man was telling me. It soon became clear that I had indeed managed to contact Denise's Dad. He was thanking her for the special place in her garden which she had dedicated to him and she appeared so touched to hear this.

The information he was giving me was clear and concise. I could not really believe it was happening but Denise was thrilled, he was passing on personal details that I could never have known.

As the reading was progressing Denise suddenly asked me to ask her Dad about the important date in their family history. Now several things at once occurred here. At precisely the time Denise was asking me to get this date I suddenly felt as if I was in the Sea. All I could see, completely surrounding me were waves and the sea as far as I could see in each direction. I was freezing cold and I was absolutely terrified!

This vision could not have lasted more than a couple of seconds because as Denise finished speaking my mind was wondering how on earth on my first attempt at a reading she was expecting me to be able to come up with something as specific as a date. This was really my first experience of how the information was received in my mind. It would seem that I am capable of thinking at exactly the same time as I am receiving information. So in a nutshell at precisely the same moment, I was listening to what Denise was asking me, I was thinking that this was a lot to ask and I was experiencing this vision so three things were happening in my mind simultaneously.

The vision was so fleeting that I ignored it, mainly because the other two things were also going on in my mind. We carried on with the reading and when it was over I remembered Denise's question. I asked her what she had been referring to and her answer blew me away. She calmly stated that her Grandfather had been a survivor of the Titanic Disaster......... It took me some moments to recover from hearing this.

31

Once I had explained to Denise and Paul the vision I had seen. They were both aghast, of course they believed me because they both know me well enough to know that I would not make up such a thing. But I had learnt my first lesson; that as soon as I receive information, in whatever form, I must pass it on. Had I been doing a reading for a stranger there would be no point telling what I had seen after they had given me details of their loved ones past, because it would seem that I was not telling the truth.

Surprising News

It has not taken us long to decide that we would like to live together. Not a totally easy decision for Paul because he has two boys Daniel and Nathan living in Cambridge and although they are now young men it will not be easy putting an hours car journey between them and himself. We have talked about it long and hard and it seems the easiest way for us to be together is for him to come to Essex. Paul has put out feelers at work to find out whether he could transfer to the Anglia Ruskin in Chelmsford. It is the Sister University to the Cambridge one and therefore he would still be employed by them but just working on a different site. The University has agreed and have said that they thought he would transfer around November time.

This is good timing for us as we will have been together virtually a year by then and it would also give Paul plenty of time to sort things out with his present situation where he is living with Daniel. But today we have had a bit of a shock. The University have told him that he can have his transfer but it will have to be in June or it may not happen at all....... We will have been together 6 months! However as they have stipulated it is June or possibly never we really have no choice but to take the plunge.

Life seems to be moving so fast. My ex-husband and I have agreed to sell our family home. He is now living with his new partner and therefore it seems to be the right time. And so we are off to pastures new. It has all been a bit of a whirlwind. Finding a house to rent with Paul and my three Sons has been a stressful time but we have found somewhere albeit a fair way from Boreham. Although it is a relief to have found a suitable house, I feel dreadful at making my Sons leave the house and the village they have lived in all their lives. We all know that this is a new start and we need to look forward and it helps that they have plenty of contact with their Dad and so hopefully this move will not be too much of an upheaval for them.

Madeleine

May 2007

Paul and I have now been seeing each other for 4 months. In a strange way it seems like we have always known each other, we are so in tune and very much in love. Having him around seems to have intensified all of the paranormal occurrences that go on around me. He has certainly helped me to 'Open Up' to so much more than I ever would have imagined.

As I have said I have my own small business and part of that is to attend Breakfast Networking Meetings as a stand in for various businesses who employ me for this purpose. This always means an early morning so I spoke to Paul earlier than usual and got myself ready for bed. I was not sure how long I had been asleep but I woke suddenly, I had been having a nightmare, rare for me and it was one of those dreams that was instantly forgotten on waking. I took myself off to the loo and then got back into bed. I lay there for a few minutes wide awake. Paul was working nights so I decided to give him a call just to say hi. We chatted for a while and then I said I had better get to sleep as I had an early start. I laid down and closed my eyes and as I did so I had the most peculiar feeling that I was trapped under a bush. I could see branches all around and above me and I felt very afraid. The picture suddenly changed and I was above the bush which was covered in red berries but I did not recognise the bush as the berries were bigger and a different red to anything I have seen in England. Slowly the picture I was looking at panned backwards and I realised it was not a bush but a hedge. The hedge was running alongside a ditch. This ditch was unusual to me because it appeared to be man-made with a concrete lip.

I realised I was standing on a gravel track. It could be described as a road but if it was a road it was very rough and un-made. The road, as I looked along it, rose slowly up a hill and bore round to the right of me. Turning to see the top of the hill behind me where the road was headed, I could see what looked like either a very large shrine, gothic style or the entrance to a church. What was odd about it was that I could not see it fully. It looked too big to be a shrine and yet I had the feeling that the back of the church was missing, maybe a ruin.

The whole time this picture was unfolding before me, over and over again I was hearing the word "Madeleine." I opened my eyes in utter panic. I felt what I had just seen was very relevant and I did not know what to do. I had heard on the news that a child was missing and her name was Madeleine but I knew no more than that, I confess I had not really listened I had just heard that bit of information. Had I had some sort of message about her? In my panic my first instinct was to call Paul. He was surprised to hear from me as I literally had only rung off 5 minutes before.

"Are you ok Sweetheart?" he asked concern sounding in his voice.

"I am not sure, I have just had the strangest experience"

"You only rang off five minutes ago" he laughed, "You have not had time to experience much"

I told him the whole story.

"You need to go with your gut on this one Darling" he told me calmly. He has such a way with him, one of the things I love about him is that he can be so silly and funny and can have me in stiches but he can be such a source of comfort and guidance when the need arises.

"Why not sleep on it and see how you feel in the morning, there is certainly nothing you can do in the middle of the night."

"Ok, you are right." I agreed, "I will see what is said on the news in the morning."

I laid back down and closed my eyes. Sleep was a long time coming as the events of the night kept rolling around my head.

Morning came and I could not get to the television fast enough to put on the early morning news. They touched on the story briefly stating that the little girl who it transpired was missing in Portugal had still not been found.

My head was spinning as I got ready for my meeting. Once in the car I put the radio on, desperate to hear any fresh news. The drive to the Golf Club where the meetings are held is mainly on country roads. As I was driving I did something I had never done before. I spoke out aloud to the spirits.

"Ok, if you need me to do something with this information, you need to show me a sign"

I have had paranormal occurrences happening around me all of my life and never before had I felt the need to speak to them aloud. And so I waited, expecting a cloud of white Doves to pass in front of the car or something equally celestial.

Nothing happened and I felt dreadfully disappointed, I really felt I should be reporting what I had seen.

I suddenly realised that my radio was not on and yet I knew for certain it had been on as I was listening for the News. As I glanced at the radio the screen suddenly lit up but instead of the radio it switched to CD player and started to play at full volume. It was so loud and such an unexpected shock that I almost lost control of the car. I turned the volume down and tried to take in what had just happened.

Well I asked for a sign and there it was. My mind was made up. I needed to go to the Police.

After the Breakfast meeting was over I headed straight into Chelmsford town centre. I was very pleased to be wearing my business suit. I somehow hoped it made me look less of a nutcase. I entered the station and spoke to the officer at the main desk.

"I am a psychic medium and I think I may have some information on the little girl who is missing in Portugal." I think this was the first time I had ever said to someone that I was a medium. He smiled encouragingly at me which was a great relief and asked me to take a seat. A few minutes later an officer came out and took me to a side room.

"Thank you for coming in, we always take information from Psychics, we have found a lot of their information very useful in the past and therefore we are happy to take your statement." I went through exactly what had happened the night before, making it very clear that I had been wide awake and chatting to Paul seconds before it had happened.

"So what happens now?" I asked.

"All information we receive is passed to the Leicester-shire force who are dealing with the case as that is the area that the family lives. I doubt very much you will hear from them. Your statement will be e mailed out to Portugal where the child is missing. You are only likely to hear from them if they need any further information other than that you have already provided."

And that was that. I left the station feeling rather peculiar. I had the strongest feeling that I wanted to get on the first plane to Portugal and find her myself but of course that would be impossible, I just had to sit back and see what happened next by watching the News and reading the papers.

As you would imagine I became a little obsessed with the story, watching every News bulletin that I could, waiting for some news of that poor child. I even tried convincing myself that it could not have happened and that I had imagined it but the picture in my mind of the hedge, the ditch, the unmade road, the hill leading up to the shrine all were so clear. I was awake and I had a vision; of that I was certain.

I realised eventually that I needed to stop obsessing over it as it was doing me no good and there was nothing more I could do.

Phoebe

Discussing all my weird and wonderful happenings with Paul means I am learning all the time. He is so fascinating, he seems to know so much about the Paranormal. I am beginning to realise that I never look too deeply into anything, I seem to drift along just accepting what is happening to me. I love to read, I have done since a very young age but I do not read books which might enlighten me to certain subjects. I confess I am beginning to feel very uneducated. One thing that has always come naturally to me is to accept and believe that there are spirits around me. Maybe because it has always been the case and I have never known any different I find it so easy to accept.

Over the past couple of weeks I have had so much going on in my head, what with the sale of the house and finding somewhere to rent, Paul's imminent transfer and on top of all of that the sudden realisation that I am a medium which believe me is no small discovery. I confess it is troubling me more than anything else really. Mainly because I do not know what I am meant to be doing with this gift. It spins round and round my head. Why would this happen to me? I am not important, I am not overly intelligent so what am I supposed to be doing? Should I be helping people? The questions are endless.

I became aware today of a little girl spirit around me. I am not sure of her age, maybe six or seven. She is dressed in a little raggedy dress which is plain and shapeless. Her little face is beautiful and she has the most glorious smile. Her hair is tied up in two bunches.

She showed me some memories; mainly of her brother kicking something around in the rain, it could be a ball of some description but I am not sure. They are playing in front of some huts and he is dressed in a jacket and trousers but they are far too small for him, bless him. He looks as though they have been his clothes for years and he is rapidly growing out of them. It does not take me long to realise that these are slave children on a plantation, from many years ago. I never question why these spirits suddenly show themselves I just mentally welcome them. It is comforting to have them around.

It has been a couple of weeks since my little spirit girl arrived. She has been around quite a bit so today I mentioned her to Paul whilst chatting on the phone.

"I am not sure why she is here though" I told him.

"What is her name"? Paul asked. The words were barely out of his mouth and I heard the name Phoebe. I instantly burst into tears, I was sobbing uncontrollably and completely perplexed as to why.

"You are feeling her joy." Paul whispered, his soothing voice settled over me and the tears began to stop. "I feel she has been with you a very long time, you are feeling her joy because she is so thrilled that not only are you finally aware of her but you have her name, she is now a person to you. I am certain she is one of your guides and may well have shown herself to you to help you with coming to terms with your Spirituality." I knew he was correct, it just felt right and I have learned that this feeling of being right is to be trusted. Paul is what they refer to as a Sensitive which means he is sensitive to spirit around him, although I am pretty sure he has even more than that going on. He seems so wise, I think he has a very old soul.

I love having Phoebe with me. At times I wonder if I am imagining her, a way of coping with so much stuff going on in my life but then she surprises me by appearing when I am not thinking of her. It happened today. I had to go to the Bank in Witham. I had just come out of the Bank and I was thinking about what I had to do next, suddenly she was there, skipping along beside me. I get the strangest feeling when she appears, I begin to tingle and I feel joy and contentment. She has also taken to appearing when I am relaxing which is not very often at the moment. I love to dance, not professionally you understand, just around the kitchen or living room or wherever I happen to be when music starts to play. Today I was dusting and had the radio on. If a song comes on that makes me want to dance I am off, which generally means the housework takes ten times longer than it should. So I was dancing round the room and I became aware of her dancing alongside me. I could sense her rhythm and the way she was giving herself fully to the music. When Phoebe dances the joy in her face matches mine and we dance with unbounded enthusiasm. I never stop to wonder what people may think when I say I danced with a spirit. One of my problems is that I worry constantly about what people think and I am beginning to realise that I should just go my own way. I know what I know and it makes me happy.

The Crooked Tree

W e have moved into our new house which we are renting and Paul has transferred to Chelmsford and life seems to be settling down. I feel bad for the boys because we had to find a house in a hurry and the only one suitable for all of us is a good 20 minute drive away from the village but Matthew and Michael both drive now and I am ferrying Chris around when he needs it.

My thoughts have turned to what I am going to do for a job. I have enjoyed being self-employed and do not really want to get a job working for someone, partly because I am used to being my own boss but more so because I really do not know what I want to do. It seems crazy that at the age of 47 I still do not really know what I want to be when I grow up!

Paul has suggested a trip to Glastonbury, not the music festival I hasten to point out but the town itself. He tells me it has a very spiritual feel about it and a climb up the Tor is not to be missed as it is a very magical place. I am so excited. Somehow I feel this trip is going to be special. My Sons are all young men now and the three of them are more than capable of taking care of themselves whilst we are away.

And so we are off and I honestly cannot wait, we have booked ourselves into a little Bed and Breakfast for a couple of nights. The journey is full of laughter and quite a lot of singing. Paul has discovered my inability to sing a song using the correct lyrics and it is causing plenty of hilarity. I honestly believed that the words I was singing were the right words and he was quick to point out my errors much to my immense amusement.

Once booked in and settled we decide that a walk up the Tor would be a wonderful start to our visit. As it is June the evenings are long and we will have plenty of time.

The climb was far harder than I expected, it is incredibly steep but so invigorating. The higher we go the more energised I feel. I honestly did not believe that the energy stories were true but already I can feel something wonderful about this place. At the very top there is a Tower and I am glad to sit down once we reach it.

It is so beautiful up here, being able to see for miles in whichever direction we look. There are other people, some are taking photographs, some are picnicking and just inside the tower there is a man with a drum playing some deep and rhythmic tunes. It reminds me of Phoebe although at the moment I do not feel her presence. My mind is rushing in so many directions. Not unusual for me but I am filled with such mixed emotions, joy at where we are and of course at being with Paul but still the ever present confusion as to where this new found gift is taking me and what it all means.

Having rested we venture beyond the tower on to the top of the Tor and marvel at the view, I stand with the Sun on my face and slowly I feel myself begin to totally relax. Paul was right to suggest this beautiful place, my heart feels at home here.

As I am standing there two young ladies approach, they are barefoot and they stop close by me.

"You sensed the energy portal." The young lady speaking was smiling and looking at me with gentle appreciation.

"I am sorry," I replied, feeling a little foolish, "I do not know what you mean."

"Where you are standing is exactly where one of the energy portals are. The Tor stands in a spot where hundreds of ley lines meet. This produces an enormous amount of spiritual energy which rises up through the Tor. There are certain points where this energy can be absorbed through the portals. The way you are standing would suggest that you have naturally been drawn to this point."

"I did not know about the portals, I just felt that I wanted to stand here and absorb some of the Suns' energy." The lady nodded and went on to say....

"Take off your shoes and stand barefoot where you are. This will ground you and it will be easier to absorb the energy from the Tor. Place both of your hands over your heart and close your eyes." The woman was speaking with such certainty in her belief that I could not help but do what she was asking.

I stood for a while. I cleared my mind and relaxed. As I stood there I began to feel like something was swirling around me. I had no idea what was happening but it felt right and I was not afraid. When I eventually opened my eyes the two ladies had gone. Paul was sitting some distance away from me looking out over the fields.

I went over to him and sat down to put my socks and trainers back on.

"How was it Sweet?" He asked,

"Lovely, it was so relaxing. It felt odd because at one stage I felt like something was swirling around me but it was not scary and I felt very safe.

"I would imagine you were sensing the energy around you. Well done Babe, you really are getting into all of this now."

As we begin our journey down we chat about our experiences here. Paul felt as calm and free as I had done and we concluded that this is indeed a very special place.

"We must come back again next year." Paul smiled down at me and my heart swelled. I know I should not doubt our relationship but I cannot help it. I think it is because I have fallen so deeply in love with him that I find it hard to imagine he feels the same. He knows these thoughts cross my mind and it frustrates him, he finds it hard to know how to convince me that he is here to stay. Hearing him say that we will return helps to reassure me and at the moment that is all I can hope for.

As we near the bottom of the Tor my thoughts turn yet again to why I have been bestowed with the gift of being able to contact the other side. The way we think about ourselves can be very complex and one thing I do know is that my self-esteem is very low. I have never quite understood why this would be but it is and I have learnt to live with it but it does frequently rear its ugly head. Self-esteem and

self-confidence are two very different things as I am incredibly self-confident in a lot of ways but to believe that I am special, special enough to be able to speak to those that have passed over is a very hard thing to take in. Poor Paul, he must feel that we are going round and round in circles having the same conversation which always leaves me frustrated and confused. I decide to let the subject drop as I began to feel I was spoiling what had been a wonderful day and we headed back to the Bed and Breakfast as the Sun began to set.

It is day two of our trip and today is as beautiful as yesterday. We have just had a superb breakfast and I am feeling very spoilt. The Landlady of the Bed and Breakfast was telling us about a place called the Chalice Well Gardens. She felt that it was somewhere we would very much enjoy so that is where we are heading for now. Apparently the Chalice Well is one of Britain's most ancient wells with archaeological proof that it has been used as a water source for over two thousand years. The well is now surrounded by gardens which offer many places for visitors to sit in quiet contemplation. The waters from the well are believed to have healing properties and there is an area where one can bathe in the waters should they choose to.

Well the Landlady was quite right, this place is quite lovely. Paul and I sat amongst the flowers and just listened to the silence which was only broken by the birds singing and the babble of the water as it flowed down through the gardens to the lower levels. In one particular part of the garden there is a spring from the well where you can drink the water. Paul took great delight in drinking some, I was not so brave. The water is an orange colour because of the high iron content and that was more than enough to put me off. We are now wandering into the area they call the Orchard, having spent some time at the well itself.

At the very back of the Orchard there is a tree, standing alone and I feel very drawn to it.

"Can we sit by this tree for a while?" I ask. I sit down very close to the tree and after a few minutes I lean against it. Something had obviously occurred during the growth of the tree which had caused it to stop growing upwards. I would imagine that whatever had befallen the tree could almost have killed it. But instead of stopping growing it had managed to stay alive and now it grew parallel to the ground.

As I close my eyes I experience a very calm feeling and I begin to tingle. Not unlike the feeling I had when I first met Phoebe. My thoughts become focused and I realise that the tree is different but still very beautiful and because it is so different, it makes it rather special. It was almost as if the tree was trying to tell me to apply that to myself and I start to see things in a new way. The world is made up of many different types of people, most are kind and generous and loving. Others are not so good and that is something about our society that we must accept. But on the whole people are good and we all have our different strengths and different gifts. I realise that we should accept our gifts whatever they may be and make use of them in the best way that we can. If we apply the story of the tree to our lives then we can see that although the tree suffered something terrible, so terrible that it could possibly have died, it had the strength to carry on. It carried on growing, albeit in a completely different direction. So in times of trouble it may be worth remembering the Crooked Tree and bear in mind that even if a problem seems insurmountable there is sure to be a new way to turn and a new way to grow.

I opened my eyes and turned to look at Paul, he was watching me and smiling. As I have said before there is something rather mystical about him and I had the strongest feeling that he knew I had just had a life changing experience.

"What did it tell you?" He asked the question as though it was perfectly acceptable to assume the tree had just spoken to me.

"I think I need to process it fully before I try to explain, but let's just say my feeling of fear and doubt have been put to rest. I could feel the tears coming but they were happy tears. I moved over to where Paul was sitting and laid my head on his chest. I needed to rest, I felt exhausted as though it had taken a huge amount of energy to make contact with the tree but exhausted or not I felt wonderful.

What Now?

Once we left the Chalice Well Gardens we went for a much needed lunch, using all that energy had left me feeling so hungry. We sat discussing all that had happened over the past couple of days and then our thoughts turned to where I could go from here. We are settled in the new house and I have completely wound down my business so now I have money in the bank but I need a job. Renting a house after owning a house with my husband has made me feel a little unsettled and insecure but my share of the money from our house is not enough to buy somewhere else, especially as I have just given up my company and therefore effectively I am not earning. Paul of course has a secure job but it still would not be enough to get a Mortgage even with my big deposit and also it does feel a little soon in our relationship to be buying a property together. Much as we are in love, we are only six months in and it seems a little soon to be making such a commitment.

We did not really come to any conclusions, partly because I feel I have no particular skills. I have an entrepreneurial streak and have on many occasions tried to start up little businesses besides the recruitment agency but nothing ever really took off and I just do not know where my passions lie. One thing we did find we agreed upon was that it would be lovely to own a place where we could bring together our love of all things spiritual. We started referring to it as 'The Place', where we would have a little tea room, a room where we could do readings (Paul likes to read the Runes) and a little shop selling crystals etc. In reality I could not see this happening but it is always good to have dreams.

After lunch we set off to explore the town of Glastonbury and what a delight that was. There are so many shops dedicated to all things spiritual that we were fascinated. In one particular shop I was looking at some truly beautiful greetings cards. I bought a couple as a germ of an idea was starting and I could not wait to set out on the road home and go through my idea with Paul.

I have to admit I can talk for England. Once I start I am on a roll and this was no exception. I had been talking non-stop for a good part of the drive home. If I have an idea, especially a business idea my mind begins shooting off in all manner of directions and poor Paul was simply having to listen to my outpouring of ideas.

In a nutshell, the cards I had seen had set me thinking. The company was called 'Leanin Tree' and they featured Angels and Fairies amongst many other things and I had never seen cards like it in our area. That to me suggested a niche. It was my intention to find the supplier of these cards and see if I could start selling them locally. Maybe I could set up a market stall with the cards and other spiritually based products such as crystals. The possibilities were endless and I was beyond excited.

As always Paul was being very supportive suggesting ideas and discussing products with me. I could not wait to get home and begin investigating.

We have been home about a week and I have not stopped. I contacted 'Leanin Tree' and they told me that they had a trade supplier in my area and gave me her number. She came to see me and showed me the range of cards some of which featured Native American Indians. I had commented to her how much I loved these particular cards and as I had already mentioned my intention to have a market stall she brought in more of her samples. It transpired that she also brought into the country original items made by various tribes. She had Dream Catchers, Peace Pipes, Smudge Feathers and so on. I was thrilled as these items were beautiful. I agreed to buy some of her products to sell on the stall.

I got in touch with Chelmsford Market and discovered that as my products were not already being sold on the market that I was allowed to have a stall there. I bought some frames and framed some of the large cards I had bought as they made fantastic pictures. The stock for the stall was coming together and I was ready to go.

Paul has made some brilliant boards for us to be able to display some of the jewellery made by the Navajo and Apache tribes and we purchased hooks to hang pictures from the top of the stall. Paul is as excited as I am. We have the advantage of him working shifts which means that on some days he will be available to do the stall with me. It was so thrilling to learn that we were going to be able to work together sometimes.

So, just three weeks since I had the idea of a market stall it is our first day, chance would have it that Paul is off and so we are here together setting up the stall. Even as we are setting up people are stopping and looking, our Indian products and the crystals are creating a lot of interest. I really need to learn more about the crystals and their healing properties. Paul seems to be in his element, he is really enjoying the day, as of course am I. The other stall holders are very supportive and have been coming over to have a chat and give advice. Life is good and we are gloriously happy.

August 2007

Despite all the excitement of the past few weeks Madeleine McCann is never far from my thoughts. In the days following her disappearance I was obsessed with what had happened to her. I watched every news bulletin I could and the feeling of wanting to go to Portugal to find her never lessened. But I kept doubting what had happened and what I had seen. I was trying to convince myself that I had somehow imagined it and was looking for ways to disprove what had happened. It occurred to me one day that the church I had seen had a Gothic look about it but I had been seeing pictures on the television and in the Newspapers of the Mother and Father of the child going to Church to pray for her return. The church in these pictures was a simple white building and it dawned on me that this was what their churches looked like, not the Gothic looking thing I had seen. I almost felt a sense of relief that what I had seen was not true and the burden of feeling a need to find her could lift.

However a seed of doubt stayed with me and eventually I decided to Google 'Gothic Churches, Portugal.' The very first picture that was displayed made my blood run cold. It was almost identical to what I had seen, goose-pimples covered my body and I had to hold back the tears. I have never been to Portugal and therefore knew this was not coming from memory. So that meant I *had* seen what I thought I had.

Today I had a bit of a shock when watching the news. A report came on about the ongoing search for Madeleine and they were saying that they were going to dig up some of the garden belonging to a suspect. The reporter was standing outside the gates to the property. As they zoomed the camera into the garden through the gate I saw a hedge with red berries, it was identical to the type of bush with red berries I had seen in my vision. Although this did not make me believe that she was buried in the garden because I saw my hedge over a ditch, it did confirm to me that the type of bush I had seen did indeed exist. This to me was just more evidence that what I had seen in my vision was somehow relevant.

A sadness overwhelmed me, that poor child, would this mystery ever be solved?

Connected Minds

November 2007

A s I have said before Paul tends to hide his light under a bushel when it comes to his spiritual abilities. We had an experience today which was thought provoking on many levels.

It all began last week. We were on the stall and I needed to pop into the town to get a couple of bits. I left Paul to run things alone for a while. When I returned he appeared to be desperate for me to reach the stall as he watched me approach. When I arrived he immediately said "you have got to get a name". Naturally I was completely confused by this particularly random statement. Paul is no stranger to random but this was very odd.

"Whose name? You are not making sense."

"I don't know whose name." He replied. "That is all I have been told, you have got to get the name, although I do know it is to do with the lady running the stall opposite us." I gazed at him feeling perplexed.

"Well if you have received a message to say that we have to give that lady a name, why did they not just give you the name to give to her?"

"I don't know!" he replied in a very agitated manner. Paul was clearly getting frustrated with me, as it seemed obvious to him that I just needed to get the name and give it to the lady. Whilst all this had been going on neither of us had noticed the lady approaching.

"Excuse me." she said as she reached the stall. "Are you two talking about me? Was there something you needed?" As I looked at her a name came into my head, it was an odd name, one which I had never heard of but I knew without a doubt it was the name I was supposed to give her. Paul began to explain what had been happening and he turned to me and made a face which clearly meant 'go on then.'

He makes me smile, such utter belief in me; I cannot be anything but totally flattered.

"Well I have heard a name but I do not know if it is real. The name is Chevelle."

To say that the lady looked stunned feels like an understatement. She simply stared at me for a few moments, then as she appeared to recover she said

"That is my Grandmothers name."

Moments seemed to pass as we all stared at each other. Eventually Paul broke the silence.

"I think you need to contact your Grandmother urgently, we have received this message for a reason."

"Yes of course I will, but she does not live here, she lives in the Caribbean."

"It does not matter where she lives." Paul insisted. "You need to contact her." The lady went back to her stall and spent the rest of the day shooting us wary looks. Not that I am surprised, it must have all seemed very odd.

The next time we were working at the Market Paul called over to the lady.

"Did you call your Grandmother?"

"Not yet" the lady replied, "I have been too busy but I did want a word with you as something weird happened the other day and I wanted to ask you about it."

"Go on" Paul encouraged, looking intrigued.

"Well, the day after you told me to call my Grandmother I was leaving my flat and one of my earrings shot out of my ear. I have worn these earrings for years and they have never fallen out but this was strange because it did not just fall out, the front part seemed to shoot out of my ear and then it happened again later on in the day". Paul looked a little smug.

"It is obvious to me. What do we use our ears for?" Before anyone could answer he carried on. "We use our ears to listen and have you listened to us? Have you called your Grandmother?" The poor woman looked to the floor as if she was being told off which to all intents and purposes she was.

"I will call her as soon as I get home this evening" she promised.

Today, as we arrived to set up our stall the lady rushed over to us.

"I just wanted to thank you both; I called my family and discovered that my Grandmother, Chevelle, has been very ill. The family have been trying to contact me but I have just changed my phone and have a new number and I had not yet informed them. They could not get hold of me and have been worried sick. Naturally I feel very guilty but I am so grateful for your intervention, my family also send their thanks."

So it would seem that for whatever reason the spirits had decided to make Paul and I work together on this one. It felt good and we spent the rest of the day talking about what had happened and marvelling over the weird and wonderful ways of the spirits.

The Place

Christmas has been and gone and it is now a full year since Paul and I first spoke. It seems incredible that we are only one year into a relationship, as so much has happened already. I am realising in my heart of hearts, that although the stall is very enjoyable for us I am never going to make my fortune. Now that Christmas has gone it is very, very quiet and today I honestly thought I was going to die of exposure. It has been freezing and although I was wearing a huge amount of layers I just could not get warm, I could feel it right into my bones and it made me feel quite unwell.

Paul and I keep going over our dreams of "The Place" and I find myself constantly fretting about paying rent on a property big enough to house Paul, myself and my Sons. I think it is because I was brought up in an owned property and then my ex-husband and I bought a house, so paying rent feels like wasted money when we could be paying a Mortgage, however as I have said before, after such a short time I was wary of purchasing a house with Paul.

I keep wondering about a pub. I have worked in various ways over the years in the hospitality industry and

I do not think it would be beyond me to run a pub. Also if I could find one big enough not only would it be a business for me but I would also have somewhere for us all to live.

I spent the first nine years of my life in Newbury Park, Ilford which was in Essex but is now part of East London. We then moved to Hatfield Peverel in Essex and this village holds a big place in my heart especially as my Mum and Dad are still in the same house I was brought up in. So imagine my complete shock when today someone told me that the pub in the village called The William Boosey was up for rent for a new tenant.

"It is meant to be! It is too much of a coincidence. Just as we were thinking of taking on a pub, one comes up in the village I love." I was talking ten to the dozen and poor Paul looked completely bamboozled, he had literally just walked through the door from work.

"We would be near Mum and Dad and the building looks huge, so I am sure there would be room for all of us to live there. It is perfect."

"It may seem perfect darling but where would we start? You have not run a pub before. Are you really sure you could do this? I love you more than I can even begin to tell you and I do trust you but you have to be sure this is the right step for us. Would you expect me to give up my job at the University? To be honest, that is not really a step I would want to take."

I took his face in my hands and smiled up at him. "It is ok, calm down, we need to talk this through thoroughly before we do anything. I am not just going to jump in feet first. Go and have your shower and change, I will get your dinner and we can discuss it calmly this evening."

With a full tummy and finally able to rest Paul smiled indulgently at me. "Come on then Sweetheart, tell me all of your thoughts."

I showed him a list of pros and cons that I had drawn up that afternoon.

"It means uprooting the boys again but to be honest I do not think any of them will mind, they will be back much closer to where they grew up and Hatfield Peverel feels nearer to civilization than where we have been for the past few months."

Paul looked thoughtful. "Do you really feel you can do this? I am only thinking of you, I would hate to see you disappointed. And of course we have to convince the brewery to let us have it."

"If I know anything about myself, it is that I can do it. Believe me, when I put my mind to something I go at it all guns blazing. I am never happier than when I am trying to juggle lots of balls at the same time. You saw how quickly I arranged everything for the stall." Paul raised his eyebrows and nodded.

"Well yes, you certainly got that up and running in an amazingly short space of time."

"I actually think I thrive on adrenalin. You said you did not want to give up your job and I agree that is a sensible safety net for you. If I took on the pub in my name you will not be tied to it and if you needed to, you could walk away at any time. It will be hard work for you doing your job and living in a pub as well but I would do my utmost to ensure you got plenty of rest time."

"I will not need to walk away Sweetheart." He said as he pulled me to him, you will make this work, I know you will and I am very much looking forward to buckling up and coming along for the ride."

I think to be honest, he knew there and then that there was really very little point objecting as I had already set my heart on it.

We chatted late into the evening about all the things that we would do with our wonderful new business but we both knew that there were many hurdles to cross before our dream became realisation. As we took ourselves off to bed my head was swimming with excitement. First thing tomorrow I would call the brewery to find out just what the chances were and I could not wait.

My hands are sweating and my heart feels like it is going to jump out of my chest. The number is ringing and in my mind I am going over and over what I am going to say.

The lady answers and I honestly feel a little faint, this is our future, the conversation we are about to have could be the start that puts us on a new road.

I explain why I am calling, I give her the name of the Pub and the village that it is in. She is quiet for a moment and then she comes back on the line to confirm that it is indeed up for rent. "There are some forms to fill in" she says "which will start off your application. I will send them to you along with documents which outline how a tenancy with our Brewery works and what would be expected of you. Once you have read through these documents and understand them fully, please fill in the application form and get it back to us as soon as you can. We will look through your application and then we will give you a call. If we wish to take your application further we will tell you at that point what your next steps are."

I could not thank her enough, I felt as though I was going to start screaming I was so excited. My tummy was doing back flips and I was tingling all over. I could not stop smiling as I texted Paul to tell him what had been said.

Not one to sit and wait, I start looking into all the ins and outs of being a tenant for a Brewery, I discover that there are courses that I would need to take and also the biggest of them all, I had to have a Personal Licence to be a Landlady. No point in getting into any of that yet, we need the go ahead from the Brewery first, so now it is a waiting game.

Fingers Crossed

The boys all took the news very well. I impressed upon them that this was nowhere near decided but I wanted them to know what we were hoping to do. As I suspected they all were very pleased at the idea of being nearer "home" and all seemed enthusiastic about the idea of running a pub. This was such a relief to me as I really wanted them to feel happy about what we were planning.

The paperwork was duly completed and returned to the Brewery as quickly as I could manage and it was not long before I received a call to say they wanted us to go and see them with a Business Plan. We had a week before the meeting and therefore I needed to get my thinking cap on as I had never prepared a full business plan before. I have had plenty of ideas over the years, one or two of which had even reached the Business Plan stage but they were just for my benefit, I had never had to actually present one before. Daunting but hugely exciting.

The day of the meeting dawned. A beautiful day which I took as a sign of good things to come. Paul and I drove down together. Although I was taking on the pub in my name I thought it was important that they met Paul as well so that they could see we were both on board with the idea.

It went really well, they seemed very supportive and talked through many aspects of our journey ahead should they decide that the pub was for us. They made it clear that they would not want us to turn the pub into a Restaurant. They were happy for us to have a small restaurant somewhere in there but that it was to mainly remain a drinking pub. I could not stress enough that I wanted to turn the pub around. It had for some years had quite a bad reputation in the village and I felt sure that I could change that. I explained that my first move would be to remove the pool table and sports T.V. Part of the problem surrounding its recent fall from grace with the neighbours was that a smoking ban had just been introduced and all smokers needed to be outside of the building to smoke which was resulting in a lot of external noise.

And now we were heading for home, our excitement levels mounting but still the nervous churning of the stomach as we now had to await their decision.

As it turned out we did not have to wait long at all. The call came within a couple of days and the joy at the news mixed with terror at what we were about to take on was overwhelming. Our first job was to return to the

Brewery and complete all the relevant paperwork. The most shocking news of all was that the date to take over the pub was just six weeks away. Sitting face to face with the Directors I managed to force my face into a look which suggested I was totally fine with this bombshell. I genuinely had not given any thought as to how long this process would take but six weeks was no time at all when I considered all that we had to undertake in that time.

Getting to know my 'New Baby'

L ife is moving faster than I have ever known before but I am in my element. My mind is never happier than when it is trying to juggle a whole host of ideas. As soon as we received confirmation from the brewery, we asked if we could have a look around the building as I needed to know how the accommodation would work and just how much needed doing to turn the pub into my vision.

It is a fantastic old building standing on the hill of the old Roman Road which led from London to Colchester. For many years the pub was called 'The Crown' but the name was changed in recent history to 'The William Boosey' named after the first recorded Innkeeper who had the Inn in the year 1641.

It looked big from the outside but once we were inside it felt a little like a maze. The ground floor, when entered from the front entrance, had a large hallway which led to another set of double doors. Once through these there was an area with a large table and benches and off from here were the toilets. Four wide stairs led into the main bar of the pub which ran almost the entire length of the front of the building with the bar to the rear opposite the windows. As you stood at the top of the stairs there was another room off to the right where the pool table and various small tables stood. To the very far end of the bar was another room set up with tables in the style of a small restaurant. A door from this room led out into the garden and also to the right of this was another small toilet.

At the end of the bar, before you entered the restaurant room there was a door which led through to a small area housing the lighting switches and the music system and a very large board covered in various bunches of keys. From this area there were two more doors one leading to a passage way and the second door leading to a very large kitchen. The passage way alongside the kitchen had cupboards and at the end were large double exterior doors and round to the right was the beer cellar. Although referred to as a cellar this area was not actually underground, in the layout of the pub it was behind the main bar area. From the kitchen there was a door which led to the rear part of the garden.

Heading back to the area by the bar there were stairs which led to the upstairs living area. The staircase was small and turned almost back on itself before you reached the top and the door which led onto the main corridors.

Stepping through the door at the top of the stairs there were three ways to proceed, to the left was the Master Bedroom which was over the kitchen area. Turning right from the top of the stairs led to the bathroom and then the office and opposite those was another bedroom. At the very end of the corridor was a further bedroom.

Turning back on ourselves and taking the passage immediately opposite the stairs door took us to some sliding patio doors to our left. These led out onto a flat roof which was being used as a garden area with patio furniture. This was the roof to the cellar area. Moving forwards from the patio doors led us to a large sitting room off of which there was a small galley kitchen and off of the kitchen area was the fourth bedroom.

We were fascinated as you would imagine. Our love of all things ghostly meant that the idea of living in such an ancient building was so exciting and we could not wait.

When you buy a tenancy of a pub you are buying all the fixtures and fittings, i.e. all the furniture, kitchen equipment, bar glasses, former stock and so the list goes on.

The downside to our visit was that the disrepair was worse than I would have imagined. Paul and I had gone into the pub for a drink before we signed the papers just so that we could have a little nosey round but of course it had not been possible to see the upstairs areas.

The Bathroom was horrible and my first discussion with Paul was that I wanted it replaced. My pot of money from the sale of the house would be able to stand it, along with replacing all of the upstairs carpet. This was, after all, going to be our home for many years to come and I was prepared to lay out some money to make it a lovely place to be.

The list of things to consider and plan before our moving date was getting ever longer. I had booked various courses for us to attend. Most importantly I needed a day long crash course for gaining a Personal Licence, without which I would not be able to be a Landlady so it was vital that I pass. The people running the course in London sent me a book to read up on before the day so that I was well prepared. I was amazed, when the time came, to find that many of the people there had been sent by their employers. For instance there was a girl from a supermarket café which sold alcohol and therefore some of the employees had to have a licence to sell it. It soon became apparent that I was the only one who had taken time to really study the book. I started to look like the class swat as I was the only one offering up answers to the questions. By the end of the day I had passed the test and was happily on my way armed with my certificate. The chap running the course explained how we would then use this to apply for our licence from our local council.

One more thing crossed off the list.

Chris, Paul and I attended a course on Health and Hygiene for the kitchen and I attended another on care of the real ale and cellar management, which included how to clean the lines that the real ale ran through from the cellar to the bar. I confess I felt a little out of my depth here. All the other candidates appeared to understand fully what the processes were and it was treated rather like a refresher course than starting from scratch. However I managed to glean enough information to get started and I was sure the Area Manager would be able to offer me some support.

One of the benefits of renting the house we are in, is that we will be able to overlap, so I have given notice that we will be leaving a few weeks after we take on the pub. This means that we will be able to prepare the pub to a decent living standard whilst still having somewhere to live. Also it makes the move nice and straight forward and gives me plenty of time to make the house spic and span before we hand back the keys.

Many people love to make lists and I am one of them but this is getting ridiculous, I have lists coming out of my ears but it is the only way to keep on top of all that needs to be achieved. Time is passing so fast but I am happy with the progress we are making.

The Massage

During all this madness Paul has suggested that I go for the massage that had been bought for me by some of my girlfriends for my Birthday in November.

It seems like a good idea as I could certainly do with a break and once we take over the pub the chances of me taking some time out are highly unlikely.

So here I am sitting in an extremely comfortable chair with a lovely young lady doing an Indian Head Massage. I have already had a back massage and this is the second part of the treat so I am more relaxed than I have been in a long time. I have even managed to keep thoughts of the pub out of my mind and I am going to great lengths to keep my mind focused on all things relaxing.

I had two of my babies using a form of self-hypnosis which had been marvellous so I am using some of the techniques to relax whilst enjoying the attention I am receiving.

Having cleared my mind as much as I can and being so relaxed I had not allowed for the fact that my mind was in the perfect state to receive messages from beyond.

As I sat there I became aware of a young man standing next to the chair, much to my surprise all he was wearing was a pair of very vivid yellow swimming shorts. My mind started to race. 'Do I just ignore him? What am I supposed to do? Surely he would not appear if he was not certain that the girl would want to hear from him.'

After a minute or two he had not gone away so I took the plunge.

"Are you interested in the Spirit World?" I asked the girl.

"Oh yes" she replied, "I am really into it."

"Ok, well I did not want to scare you but I am a Medium and I think there is someone here to see you."

Her hands stopped moving on my head and she went very still.

"Here, now?" Her voice sounded as shocked as I was feeling.

"Let me describe him to you. He is quite young, I would say early twenties and the odd thing is that he is wearing nothing except a pair of bright yellow swimming shorts."

The girl gasped. "I know who it is." She whispered.

"Well that is good, let me see if he has anything to say." I opened my mind up further to try to hear him.

I went on to tell her everything he was saying to me and it all made sense to her.

Once I had finished and he had gone the lady explained to me that he had been a family friend. The two families had spent all their time together as they were great friends. They even holidayed together and therefore the children of the two families were like brothers and sisters. This young man and the lady massaging me were children from the two different families. She explained that when they were on holiday for a couple of years running, when the young man was about 13 he had a pair of bright yellow shorts, so bright that they were a constant source of jokes for the two families.

He had lost his life in a car crash when he was in his early twenties. He had appeared wearing the yellow shorts so that she would immediately recognise him.

"Thank you so much again Judith, I never would have imagined that he would come through to me like that."

"No need to thank me, I am always thrilled to be able to pass on any messages that I can."

As I am driving home I go over all that had happened. I am forever fascinated at the spirits ingenuity when it comes to showing themselves. They appear to know that I will be able to pass on their best wishes to their loved ones and they take any opportunity they can to get through.

And so it begins

One of the many exciting factors of taking on the pub is the feeling of having a 'clean sheet' with regards to what we are going to do with the inside. I have done drawings and plans and know exactly how I want it to look. Paul has arranged to borrow an industrial carpet cleaner to clean the carpets throughout the ground floor of the pub. The brewery has spoken to the previous tenant and she has provided details for the various providers of the Sky T.V. and the games machines so that I can arrange for these to be removed. There are a couple of very large outbuildings on the property and I intend moving the snooker table out to one of them so that my boys and their friends can play on it out there. The room that had held the snooker table I am going to turn into a lounge type area. I have ordered a very snazzy, all singing all dancing, coffee machine for the bar and I intend making the lounge a coffee area with lots of lovely home-made cakes. The display cabinet for the cakes has also been ordered. My hope is that I can draw day time trade into the coffee area. So with this at one end of the pub and our little restaurant at the other end with a very large bar area in the middle I feel we have all bases covered with regards to providing the customers with the surroundings they want.

Amongst the tonne of paperwork I have had from the Brewery are the names of the existing staff who are going to be Tupe'd over to me. When someone takes over a business that already has staff the law provides the staff with protection and the new owner of the business must take them on.

Jo and I have had long conversations about the Pub. Jo has worked in bars and restaurants and is very keen to come and work with me. So with Jo, the previous staff, myself and Paul and my three boys on hand we are certainly not going to be short on help.

I have contacted all the previous staff and arranged to meet at the pub the morning after we get the keys so that we can all get to know each other and I can let them know I intend starting them back on straight away so that the hours they work until we open will be assisting with the re-decoration.

I have also decided to take on a chef. I advertised and interviewed a few and once I had made my decision I gave him his starting date and asked him to work on some menus for us to go through before our opening day so that we can get supplies ordered and some preparation done, ready for our first day.

Paul and I have been on an overnight trip to view furniture for the lounge area as the trade furniture company I had found only allowed visitors to view by appointment.

My head is almost at the point of bursting. The furniture has been ordered and everything is very rapidly falling into place. I am planning our takeover like a military operation. I have allowed 6 days from the day we get the keys until we open and believe me we have got an awful lot to do in that time.

I cannot tell you how it has been, preparing all of this in a six week period but I could not be happier. On the day that we take over we are to meet the Area Manager at 11am by which time the previous tenant should have moved out and we will be handed the keys, sign the final paperwork, the monies will have been transferred over to the Brewery to buy the business and we will be off and running. My legs go a little weak at the very thought of it.

We have had little opportunity to look at the living area and therefore our plan is to call the boys as soon as the Area Manager has left. Our first job will be to measure their bedrooms and go and order the carpet. I have already spoken to the carpet suppliers who have assured us they will be able to fit the carpet within a couple of days of ordering. We have already bought paint for the bedrooms, the upstairs living area and for all of the bar areas.

Within the pack from the Brewery is everything we need to order our first drinks delivery. That should be interesting and Jo will certainly come into her own when deciding what we need.

Day One

The universe is being kind to us and our first day dawns bright and beautiful.

I feel sick with excitement. Our new life starts today. Paul has booked holiday so that we have a week together to get everything under way.

The paperwork is all signed. The Area Manager has wished us luck and gone on his way. We have a new home and a new business. Paul and I are in the bar, arms wrapped round each other.

"I cannot believe we have done it" I whisper to him. "I have such a good feeling about this. I really feel we have found where we are meant to be, we have our 'Place'." Paul smiled down at me.

"I am so proud of you, I honestly cannot believe that you have managed to pull this all together in such a short space of time." I blushed, very much enjoying the praise.

"Well you know me, once I get a bee in my bonnet I will not stop until I have achieved what I set out to do."

The boys all arrived soon after and we set about exploring our new home. There was much excited chatter and I was thrilled to have us all together. One of the things that I found hard to bear as they all grew up was how we drifted apart. They naturally all had their own friends to be out and about with and we very rarely spent much time as a family. But now I feel that we are about to bond again, all sharing in this new adventure.

Rooms measured we went and ordered their carpet and then back to the pub for the real work to start. Chris and Mike had the rooms near the office and Matt had the room at the far end of the pub next to the galley kitchen and living room. They all went off to start painting their respective rooms while Paul began cleaning all the carpets in the pub.

My Auntie Brenda has come to stay with my Mum for a few days. Her husband, my Uncle Mickey passed away in 2005. He was connected with the pub trade his whole working life and as Mum and her sisters had been brought up in a pub this new venture is really exciting for the family and Brenda did not want to miss the chance of helping to get it all going. So they have arrived with cleaning products in hand they head off to the upstairs living area to begin massive task of cleaning.

Day Two

We met the staff this morning. Pam talked us through the bar area and the tills and Lyn showed us the kitchen. Sam, our chef was very enthusiastic at the size of the kitchen although Lyn seemed almost apologetic showing us various items of equipment which had really seen better days. This was not an expenditure I had allowed for and it seems that if we are going to have an efficient kitchen running I will need to get two new fryers and a new oven range.

The news about the kitchen really is quite shocking as those items will not be cheap to replace but according to the Brewery they are not considered as part of the building and they are my responsibility. So I have bitten the bullet and ordered them, luckily they will be in and fitted by the time we open.

The bar is also dreadfully low on stock and my first order to the Brewery is massive. I am tied in to the brewery and everything I sell behind the bar must be bought through them even the soft drinks.

The chef is the person who orders in the supplies for the kitchen and after consultation with him we put in our first order ready to set up our new menu. For the time being I am going to print the menus for the restaurant. I have a decent printer and can produce nice menus but I have asked Nick who is my son Michael's partner if he would sort out leaflets as he works for a printing firm. It is my intention to leaflet the village to let them know that the William Boosey is now a very different place to visit.

After we had talked through everything, I asked the staff if they would be willing to come in tomorrow to help with the painting and cleaning as we begin to get the place ready to open in five days.

Day Three

The energy in the place is amazing with lots of friendly chatter as the painting of the downstairs gets going in earnest. It was my intention to also help with the painting but so much is going on that I keep having to stop and answer questions or deal with deliveries. I also had to take time to order the bathroom which will be fitted next week. I am really glad that we had decided to have an overlap time with the house we are renting. It is nice to go home at the end of a very busy day to shower, eat and relax for a few hours before going back to start again.

Day Four

The lounge furniture came today. I had ensured that that area of the pub was cleaned and painted first so that it would be ready for the delivery. It took some doing getting the snooker table out but we managed it. Paul and I unpacked the furniture and got it placed exactly as I had planned. It looks fantastic and I could burst with pride. The coffee machine was installed this morning. That presented problems with the water supply to it but it all got sorted in the end. I have a bookcase at the end of the room packed with paperback books and I have made a sign saying book swap. I saw this idea somewhere and really liked it. We have purchased some board games which we have dotted around for customers to play if they wish.

Day Five

We arrived at the pub really early this morning as the dray was due with our first delivery. It has become my habit to open the main doors as soon as I arrive to let in some fresh air to try to get rid of the smell of paint. As I approached the Lobby area I could see an envelope on the floor. Too early for the postman and it was definitely not there when we left yesterday evening. I picked it up, on the front it simply said 'Judith'. Intrigued I opened it and my heart plummeted. It was from Sam, our new Chef. He was very apologetic but stated that he had decided to stay at his present job. My legs began to shake and I knew that I needed to sit down. The initial shock quickly turned to anger and concern. What were we going to do? We open in two days! I sat in the lobby area, staring into space, my mind going ten to the dozen. We can do this. I will change the menus today and we will go with 'All things home- made.' Lyn has already proven she is a marvel in the kitchen. Between us we can do it.

All the barrels are in the cellar and I have put a couple of the real ale in place ready as they have to rest for a while before pulling pints as the sediment needs to settle. Jo and I spent the entire morning getting the bar fully stocked. It is really beginning to look fantastic. Lyn has been in the kitchen all day, she really took it in her stride when I told her about the Chef. I discussed with her what we would offer and she is making Quiche and Pies and Cakes like a mad woman. I love her already!

Day Six

We are ready! This afternoon we are having a party. We have invited friends and family to join us, to thank them for all their help and support as we have made this transition. Lyn, Chris, Paul and I have been in the kitchen all morning preparing a buffet. Chris the youngest of my sons worked for a time in a local restaurant kitchen and is well versed with how it all works. He came with Paul and I to do the Health and Hygiene Course and the four of us are really bonding as a team.

Mike (my middle son) and Nick (his partner) are going to help behind the bar this afternoon. That will be perfect for them as they are both incredibly sociable. They shouldn't have to do much as the staff are going to be here as well but the more the merrier. I am so excited.

On our very first day in the pub I noticed that at the top of the stairs, where you can either turn right into the lounge area or head straight on into the bar, there was a very odd cold spot. I had looked around to see what might be causing it but there was nothing to explain it. Whenever I walked into that particular area I felt as though I was not alone. I had asked Paul to go and see if he felt anything in that part of the pub. I did not explain where it was and sure enough he found it. He showed me the exact same spot as I had noticed and said he did not feel comfortable when he stood there. We decided between us that someone was not happy with our presence there. Maybe the resident spirit did not like change.

Today, I was just putting the final touches to the bar and as I walked around the entire ground floor checking that everything was ready for this afternoons celebrations I noticed that the cold spot was not there. I moved around the area but simply could not find it. If anything I now felt a real sense of warmth and calm there. I went and found Paul and asked him to go and stand in the cold spot. I watched him go and saw that he appeared to be having the same problem I had. He wandered around looking perplexed.

"I cannot find it Sweetheart." He suddenly stood very still, looking thoughtful. I walked over to him, he took me in his arms and smiled.

"Can you feel it?" he asked.

"Feel what?" I replied, although I suspected I knew exactly what he was going to say.

"It has gone, but now I feel really relaxed and happy standing here. I think they have accepted us". I snuggled into his chest and smiled.

"Exactly what I felt." I replied and I knew that everything was going to be fine.

The Next Chapter

The party was a huge success and we are now into our fourth week. Once we had the pub open and running I spent several days cleaning the house before we made the move across to the pub. Once we had moved completely I did the finishing touches to the house and we handed back the keys.

The new bathroom has been fitted and the upstairs of the pub is now our lovely new home. The boys are all settling in nicely and seem happy to be back in the area they grew up in.

Matthew my eldest helps me clean the pipes for the real ale. We do this once a week and it is lovely to spend time with him. It is such a pleasure having the boys all involved in their own particular ways within the business.

We leafleted the village and we have a steady flow of customers coming to 'check us out'. We have inherited some regulars from the previous tenants who are a lovely group and seem happy with the changes we have made.

I have settled into a routine of getting up early to clean the pub before the day starts. I then tend to flitter from place to place. I help Lyn in the kitchen as I decided to forget the idea of a chef for the time being; we seem to be managing and the customers appear to like the home cooked food. I do not do too much bar work as Pam and Jo handle most of that with Amy doing shifts as well but there is so much else to do I am busy from dawn till dusk which is just how I like it.

Paul is back to work, which if I am honest I think he was pleased about. It must have been nice for him to get back to a bit of normality.

On one of his days at home between shifts I talked to him about our left over stock from the market stall that was boxed up in one of the outbuildings. It seemed such a shame to just leave it there and it could be bringing in a little more money for us. So we decided to display it at the end of the restaurant and see how it went and so far it has been selling well.

We did have another shock: just a couple of weeks after opening I had a fire safety inspection. I was told by the fire service that the extractor fans in the kitchen were so clogged up with fat that they were an extreme fire hazard and would need to be professionally cleaned. I was told it looked as though they had not been cleaned for years. As you can imagine I was horrified but what really baffles me is how previous tenants have been getting away with not putting this sort of thing right. So as usual I did the right thing of course, I was not going to risk my business and family by not dealing with it. Once the professional cleaning firm who specialise with this type of cleaning were booked I had to close for the day because of the fumes and we all had to stay well away from the kitchen area whilst the process was carried out. Another huge expenditure I had not expected or allowed for.

Lyn and Pam had told us that there were meant to be two ghosts in the pub. One who seemed to walk up and down behind the bar and previous staff had apparently talked of being pushed. There was also supposedly a strange feeling in the lobby area between the kitchen and the bar. This is a funny little area of no man's land. The audio equipment for supplying music to the bar is here as well as all the switches for all the lighting. A big board housing all the different keys and general storage for bits and bobs. This is where the stairs lead up from to go to the living area and three separate doors lead to the bar, the kitchen and the passage which leads to the cellar area.

This morning I was sorting through the CD's for the pub. I had bought a selection of new ones, some which were just gentle music which were ideal for certain times of the day. We have a knitting group who have adopted us as their meeting place so this music is perfect for the morning once a week that they are in the coffee area.

As I was sorting through them I was humming to myself. Paul and the boys had all gone off to work and

Lyn and Pam had not yet arrived so I had the building to myself.

Suddenly I heard a lady muttering. I could definitely tell it was female and for a moment I thought Lyn had come in and I had not heard the back door. I went into the kitchen but it was empty. I went back to the lobby and stood for a moment listening. There it was again. When I first learnt how to do a reading Paul taught me to 'open up'. It is just a method of clearing the mind and allowing the spirits to speak to you. I am still getting used to it but when I do it, I would almost describe it as throwing a switch in my mind. So I closed my eyes and allowed myself to see. And there she was; a little woman, she reminded me of the type of lady portrayed in period dramas, the cook in the kitchen all rosy cheeked and homely looking. She was just smiling and staring at me, she then started to speak but I simply could not understand what she was saying; it was just muttering as though she was talking quietly to herself. I stood there for a while but nothing further was happening. She was not moving, she was just smiling and occasionally muttering so eventually I said out loud that it was lovely to meet her but I had to get on with my work and I allowed my mind to close. It was such a nice experience and I felt a warm glow for the rest of the morning.

I heard on the news this morning that it is a year since Maddie went missing and still there is no trace of her. My heart weeps for her. I am so certain that she has passed away and a huge part of me wants to go and look for her, to enable them to bring her body home. It just shows how powerful my experience was, that a year later I can remember every aspect of it so clearly and still have such strong feelings about it. Hopefully someone took a little notice of the information I gave them but there really is nothing more I can do.

Nerves Setting In

We hosted a 40th Birthday party last night. It was fabulous, such a good atmosphere in the pub and as you can imagine we took a fortune over the bar. The customer who booked the party was thrilled, the buffet went down a storm and the D.J. I hired for the event was brilliant. This morning I was buzzing but as the day progresses I begin to think about the difference between what we took last night in relation to our usual daily takings which are not high. It has only been a couple of months but I feel a little worried. I have ordered a banner to display outside the pub. I have also spent hours filling all the flower baskets along the front of the pub and I know it will look fantastic once they begin to hang. My Dad regularly comes to tend to the garden which is looking lovely. I think he really enjoys it, he has always loved gardening and he seems happy to be making a contribution towards making the pub a success.

We have had a lot of comments over the past couple of months about the lack of better known lagers. As I have said before we have to stick rigidly to only buying from the Brewery and they only do their own lager on tap. Of course the Brewery do also supply bottled lager but most customers seem to prefer lager off the tap. I have had several people say to me that 'everyone buys out', meaning that even though they are tied into the Brewery they still buy in barrels etc. from cash and carry. Obviously they are so much cheaper from there and therefore this would help to improve profits but it really is not me to do anything that I feel I shouldn't, so I am sticking to the rules. However as things are at the moment we are not making a profit. The overheads and of course all of the initial expenditure I had, mean that the pot of money is virtually gone and we need to start making a profit soon.

I think part of the problem is that I am spending too much of my time in the kitchen which had never been my intention, it makes me feel as though I am losing control of the reins and that if I were able to spend more time devoted to the business I could see where we needed to make some changes to pull in the customers. Therefore although I can ill afford it I have decided to take on a cook. I did not advertise for a chef as I simply cannot afford the higher wages but a cook would free me up from the kitchen and we would still be able to put out the food that we are doing. After a few interviews I have found a very nice chap named Alec who can start immediately so I am hoping things will now pick up a bit.

The Funeral Man

It is a beautiful July morning and we have just opened. Jo and I are chatting in the bar and a gentleman and two ladies walk in.

"Are you able to do a wake for a Funeral?" The man asks.

"Yes of course." I reply. "Please follow me."

I take them to the lounge area and we sit down to discuss what they need. In this part of the lounge I have three, two-seater settees, all facing into the coffee table in the centre. I sit on one, the two ladies sit opposite me and the man sits on the one between us to the left of me. The two women with him look considerably younger than him so I presume they are his daughters. As we are chatting the man keeps referring to 'her'.

"Was this your Mother?" I ask. For a moment he does not speak....

"No, my wife, she had a brain tumour." He whispers. He put his head down and tears start to pour down his cheeks. No one moves. Gently I put my hand to his face. I cup my palm under his chin and begin stroking his face with my thumb. Still no one speaks. Deep inside my mind a little voice is asking if it is appropriate to be stroking the face of a complete stranger but it feels right and I carry on until he stops crying. I took my hand away and asked if he was ok.

"Yes, sorry." He replies.

"Don't be sorry, it is perfectly understandable….. So, I think I have all I need, if you have any questions or want to make any changes to what we have discussed this is my card, just give me a call."

As they leave I go back to Jo in the bar.

"Well that was very odd, I just stroked that blokes face because he was crying, it felt really strange, almost like a dream for a moment and nobody said anything or seemed to think it was an odd thing for me to do."

"You are funny." Laughed Jo. "I never know what you are going to do next!"

At that moment customers enter the bar and we are back to business.

Two weeks have passed since my 'Funeral Man' came in and today is the day of the Wake. The lounge area has been re-arranged so that they have that area to themselves, the buffet is all laid out and we have roped off the lounge with a sign saying private function. The bar is packed. Jo, Amy and Pam are running the bar and Chris is working with Lyn and Alec, our new cook, in the kitchen to keep the buffet topped up and do any meals that are needed in the restaurant. I am feeling really happy. I am never happier than when I am rushing from place to place ensuring all is running smoothly.

It is now late afternoon and the pub is virtually empty, only a final few members of the family remain. I am in the lounge clearing down the buffet when a young man comes up to me.

"Are you the Landlady?" He asks. My heart sinks. I thought it had all gone so well but I feel he is about to complain.

"Yes I am." I reply, waiting for what is to come next.

"When my sisters came to arrange the funeral with my dad, you touched my dad's face when he was crying." To say I am shocked by this would be an understatement.

"Yes I did." I reply, unsure what else to say.

"This may seem odd." He says. "But could you please do to me what you did to my dad"

I stare at him for a moment processing what he has just asked but I am never one to shy away from anything and so feeling slightly daft I put my hand to his face, cup his chin in my palm and begin stroking his face with my thumb. Tears appear in his eyes and I take my hand away.

"Thank you." He laughs slightly, clearly now embarrassed. "My sisters told me what happened but I just had to see it for myself. Ever since we were tiny, if any of us were upset my mum would cup our chin in her hand and stroke our face with her thumb until we were calm again, she did it with everyone, not just us." Goosebumps started to rise up all over me. He carried on speaking. "When they saw what you did they knew that my mum had somehow used you to comfort my dad and I just wanted to say thank you as it meant the world to all of them and now of course me too" My throat has gone dry and tears are threatening. As I stare at him completely unsure of what to say he suddenly grabs me in a bear hug, then just as quickly before I have had a chance to say a word he walks away.

I stand for a moment as a warm feeling spreads through me. I have been told in the past by Mediums that I am what is known as a 'Trance Medium'. One who has the ability to allow the spirits to enter the body and effectively take over, using the Mediums body as their own. I admit I have never taken much notice but from what I understand this might be exactly what happened with this lady. From the Spirit World she needed to comfort her husband. She knew I could do it, even though I was not really aware of it myself, so she took her chance and used me as a channel to her husband. We learn something new every day and I am thrilled to discover that this is something I can do, as it undoubtedly brought this family some comfort and that is good enough for me.

Finding More Customers

We are into our fifth month. Alec is doing ok in the kitchen although I am worried about his time keeping and his rather blasé attitude to work but we shall see how it goes. I am also still very worried about the level of our takings, what we are taking in no way matches the outgoings and we simply cannot keep running at a loss. After the successful events we have had, I have suggested to Paul that we try and push that aspect of what we do. I have a good D.J. to use. We always put on a fabulous buffet and I know I can arrange just about anything I am asked. So with that in mind I decided to once again leaflet the village.

As we are going to be leafleting about our events I have decided to kill two birds with one stone and also advertise an event at the pub for a local charity. It will be nice to raise money for them but at the same time hopefully it will draw plenty of people in from the village who will then get to see what a nice venue we now have.

I have asked the Blue Falcons if they would be good enough to come along and do a small display in our garden. We are going to have stalls, a barbeque and some other entertainment. I am really looking forward to it and praying for good weather. It is a bit of a gamble to have the event in August. The weather is more likely to be good but a lot of people might be on holiday, however I cannot put everything on hold simply because people may not be around, so August it is.

I have been keeping an eye on the weather forecast and am thrilled to see that Saturday is going to be fine. Arrangements for the event are all in place and I am so looking forward to it.

Jo has asked if she can have more hours and I understand why but I am loathe to have any more expenditure at this time as we are really starting to struggle financially. I never envisaged this situation and I feel rather foolish, I was so sure trade would pour in. I have been reading that the smoking ban has had a very bad effect on the pub trade. The ban came in just before we took on the pub and at that point it had not really started to show as being a huge problem for pubs. In addition to this the Supermarkets have started to sell alcohol at much cheaper levels than ever before and it is becoming the new normal, especially with the youngsters, to have a few at home before hitting the pubs and clubs. Not good news for our trade at all.

The day of the event arrives and I am up at the crack of dawn. In addition to all the normal morning cleaning jobs we have the stalls to set up in the garden, the food to prepare and I feel a bit tired before we even start which is not good. Usually at such times adrenalin kicks in and there is no stopping me but I think worry about our trade is putting extra stress on me and I am not sleeping as well as I usually would. As the day progresses I have to keep leaving what I am doing to go and assist with other jobs and my temper is starting to fray. This is not like me at all and I am feeling a little concerned.

Finally, whilst in the kitchen, Jo says something to me and I snap, I yell at her and Jo being Jo yells right back. Even as it is happening I am astounded. I never behave like this, I simply do not lose my temper and I certainly do not shout at anyone especially Jo who I love with all my heart. Two women cannot go through times together that we have and not have a very close bond. I run from the kitchen and out to the back of the garden to try and regain some composure. But there is nowhere to hide because just at that moment the Blue Falcons Lorry pulls into the back yard and members of the team start pouring into the garden.

Martin, one of the male members of the support team sees me and realises something is wrong. He takes me to a quiet corner of the garden and calms me down.

"This is not me, you know it isn't." I say to him and he nods as he puts a comforting arm around my shoulder.

"Just stop for a moment and consider what you have been doing for 6 months now. You have been working non-stop to make this a success. You must be tired. Maybe after this weekend you should consider a little break, just to give you a breather so that you can come back and start afresh." I know what he is saying is true and I hug him as I thank him for his words of comfort.

I went back to the kitchen to find Jo. I took her away from the bar for a moment and apologised for my behaviour. It would take more than that though to break our friendship and we end up crying and laughing all at the same time.

Although we have had a lovely day I am yet again disappointed at the turn out from the village. We had plenty of supporters of the Blue Falcons and friends and family turned out once again for us but I begin to wonder just what I have to do, to begin to make this pub a success. We have however made enough to be able to make a good donation to the charity and for that I was very grateful and relieved.

Spiritual Shocks

Although the pub is not as busy as I had hoped by this time; my days are extremely busy which means I barely have time to think but over the past few days I keep hearing the word 'Shaman' spoken to me. Considering how much I like to read I am amazed that I have not come across this word before. I told Paul and asked him if he had heard of the word. He said he had and he explained that a Shaman is someone who is like the Medicine Man of a tribe, the story teller, generally held in high esteem, a Shaman usually has the ability to heal and has a very strong connection to the Spirit World.

"Why do you think I keep hearing the word?" I asked Paul.

"Maybe they are trying to tell you that you are a Shaman." He smiled gently. "It would not surprise me Sweetheart, I have always said I feel there is something special going on with you."

Well that idea came as a bit of a shock. As I have explained previously I do not have a very good sense of self-esteem and now once again it was being suggested that I was someone with a special gift. It all seems very hard to imagine and it made me feel as odd as I did when I first discovered my gift as a Medium.

A couple of weeks have passed since Paul suggested that I may be a Shaman and now we are off again to Glastonbury. Our trip last year was such a success and I cannot wait to be back there. Everything is running smoothly at the pub and I trust everyone implicitly so after the frantic pace of the past few months I have taken Martin's suggestion and we are treating ourselves to two nights away.

I admit I feel a little strange having a treat when the pub is struggling so badly but Paul has insisted. Although he pays his way in the pub he does have a little in reserve and so I give in and let him pay for this break. I think he deserves it too as he is working full time and spending many a long hour working in the pub.

We enjoy the drive and as usual we chat and laugh. It is so good to just be in each other's company again, just the two of us. Our relationship is still so young and it will do us good to be alone.

After a good night's rest at our Bed and Breakfast we cannot wait to climb the Tor once again.

We make it to the top and as last year it was totally worth the climb. It is a beautiful day and we are enjoying the Sun and the cool breeze and the totally incredible views. Since my gift was discovered Paul loves to test me and today it seems is no exception.

"I want you to try something." He says as we stand taking in the view.

"Do you see that thing over there in the gap in the trees?

"The tall thing that looks like a radio mast or something similar?" I asked.

"That's it, yes. I want you to see if you can travel over there in your mind and see what it is."

"What on earth are you talking about?" I asked feeling totally perplexed.

"It is called Astral Travel, there is an awful lot about it on the internet and I just wondered, given the gifts you have whether you would be capable of such a thing."

Not wanting to disappoint him I said I would give it a go.

"Stand with your feet slightly apart so that you are comfortable." Paul directed. "Close your eyes and relax, concentrate on the tall thing and see what you can see."

I did as he asked and the strangest thing happened. As I closed my eyes it was as if the Sun came out and in front of me I could see what looked like a tomb. It was oblong in shape, it appeared to be concrete and I could see that on the side there was either a plaque or wording that was engraved into the concrete. I studied it for a moment or two but then realised this could not possibly be the tall thing I had been trying to see. I opened my eyes and as I did, out of the corner of my eye I saw the tower on the top of the Tor. I staggered and almost fell as it completely threw me. Paul grabbed my arm as I started to fall.

"Are you OK?" He asked concern covering his face.

"Yes I am fine, I just was thrown a bit as I opened my eyes as I thought the tower was behind us."

"Ahhh." He nodded, a satisfied smile lighting up his face. "Well if you had been over there looking at whatever that is, the tower would most definitely have been behind you."

"An interesting theory, I have to agree but unfortunately I do not know what I was looking at but it was not that, it was a tomb of some description."

"Oh I see." Disappointment clouded his eyes. "I was so sure you would be able to do it."

I hugged him. "Never mind," I said "even if I had seen something tall, how would we have ever known that I had gone and looked at that, as we do not actually know what it is." He agreed that I was right about that and we wandered over to look at the stainless steel plinth at the opposite end to the tower. We had not looked at this the previous year, I think there were too many people around it so we did not bother.

It was engraved with the points of the compass and pointed out various landmarks and Counties that you can see from the top of the Tor on a clear day.

As we studied it I suddenly noticed that one of the landmarks noted was the Hood Monument. Paul's surname is Hood.

"Goodness me! Look at this Paul, there is a Hood Monument. We really should try to go and see it whilst we are in the area."

"Sounds like a plan" he grinned, "shall we try and find it tomorrow?"

The following day we headed into town. I wanted to try and find a shop selling Ordinance Survey maps where hopefully I could trace the Hood Monument. I have a real thing about maps, I love to read them and therefore I was thrilled to be looking for a new one. We were in luck. I found the map that I thought would do the trick and was studying it in the shop.

"Are you looking for anywhere specific?" The young man behind the counter asked.

"Yes, the Hood Monument, we understand it is in the local area somewhere"

"I know what will make life easier, I will see if I can find it on the internet." After a few moments searching he smiled in satisfaction. "Got it. It is in a village called Compton Dundon, which is on the map you are looking at." Thanking the man profusely for his help we purchased the map and set off.

We reached the village and asked a walker if they knew where the monument was and they told us where we could park and walk up through the woods. I led the way excited to find it but I could never have expected what was about to happen.

The trees suddenly opened out into a clearing and there right in front of me was the tomb I had been looking at yesterday in my "Astral Travel" experiment. I instantly burst into tears, the shock of seeing it, too much for me. My immediate thought was that I had had a premonition of what I was going to see today. Paul caught up with me and I turned and he wrapped me in a hug as I sobbed uncontrollably. Naturally he was completely confused as to why I would be behaving in this way.

As soon as I managed to get myself under control the words burst out of me. "It is the tomb! The one I saw yesterday in my mind, when we were on the Tor."

Paul gasped and stared at me in confusion, then he looked up and a look of complete wonder passed over his face.

"Look" he said "you did it."

When I turned the full understanding of what had happened began to sink in. As I entered the clearing I had been so shocked at the sight of the tomb that nothing else registered with me but there on top of the tomb was the pillar.

This pillar was very similar to Nelson's Column in Leicester Square, London which is a pillar with a statue of Admiral Nelson at the top, this one however had what looked like a boat at the top. We moved forward and began to read the inscription carved into the base of the monument. A plaque exactly as I had seen. The monument is dedicated to Sir Admiral Hood and has been there since 1831.

I could not begin to tell you how I was feeling. How was it possible that I had come here yesterday in my mind and looked at the base of this monument? As if to prove once and for all that that was indeed what had happened Paul told me to turn round. There behind me was the cut in the trees and through the gap we could see the Tor, roughly five miles away.

We sat for a while and discussed what had happened although to be fair on my part it was just going over and over it in complete disbelief. What struck me as particularly unbelievable was the way the events had joined up to lead us here. Had we not bothered looking at the plinth at the top of the Tor we would not have found out about the Hood Monument. At the time that we decided to visit the monument we had absolutely no idea it was in any way connected to what we had tried earlier on the Tor. It all was just so incredible but if I thought that was the end to the days' shocks I couldn't have been more wrong.

Once back to the car I studied the map, looking for somewhere else to go for a wander. I found another wood on the way back towards Glastonbury so we decided to head there.

It was such a beautiful day and as we began the climb through the woods a calm descended over me and the shock of what happened earlier began to ease off. Once again I was leading the way up a steep path and as I walked a tingling feeling started to pass over me. To the left of us the woods dropped away and we could see over the fields but to the right the woods climbed towards the summit which at this point we could not see.

"Jude!" Paul spoke in a hushed voice as he called for my attention. I paused and turned to look at him.

"Are you feeling anything in here?"

"Funnily enough yes." I replied "I was feeling tingly just now but I have a strange feeling that there is something special about this place."

"Open up" he said "I think you will get a surprise."

Well that was the understatement of the year. As I allowed my mind to open I became aware of what can only be described as Fairies, Elves, Imps, all manner of little people all around. I stood perfectly still, stunned by what I could see. They were all staring at me but the most peculiar thing about it was that they appeared to be looking at me with a kind of reverence. This I found almost more disconcerting than the fact that I was looking at creatures I would never have believed truly existed. They were all to the right of us in the woods, as far as I could see as the woods rose up the hill. But the shocks did not end there. Towards the back of the wood further up the hill I saw a Centaur. As he looked at me I concentrated on him fully, momentarily putting all thoughts of the other creatures out of my mind. I knew instinctively that this creature was going to be very special for me but at that point I did not know why.

I do not really know how long I stood there for but eventually I turned to Paul.

"What can you see?" I asked him. Not willing to say what I could see, I felt he would think I was crazy.

"Woodland creatures" he smiled "do you see them?"

How I did not faint I shall never know. Until that moment I really believed my mind was playing tricks on me but he could see them too and I had given absolutely no indication of what I was seeing. "Can you see the Centaur?" I asked. Paul looked shocked and looked all around. "No, where is it?" I pointed to where I could see him standing but Paul could not see him at all which rather confirmed my feeling that he was special to me.

As we carried on up the path through the woods, the creatures all stood and watched. We reached the summit and entered a clearing at the top of the hill. We went and sat on a sunny patch of grass and talked over what we had just seen. My mind was reeling. What a day!

Eventually we decided it was time to go down and find somewhere to have something to eat. As we went down through the woods neither Paul nor I could sense the creatures. For whatever reason the moment had passed and they had either left the woods or they had chosen to once again hide their presence from us.

Several days later back at the pub I was busily working behind the bar before we opened and I suddenly became aware of the Centaur. It is hard to describe exactly how I could feel him but I knew he was there and at the same time I sensed two Sprites. The Centaur spoke to me and explained that he would be staying with me as a protective spirit. He almost seemed to be apologising for the presence of the Sprites saying that when I visited the wood they decided they wanted to come with me. He had known I would be coming and that he would be staying with me as a protector but the Sprites were just with me because they wanted to be.

My life just seems to get stranger and stranger but if I am honest I love it and would not have it any other way.

Autumn

Our lovely restful trip to Glastonbury was only a couple of weeks ago but it seems a lifetime as I have thrown myself back into pub life. Jo has once again mentioned upping her hours. It is difficult as she is such a good friend but I honestly cannot afford to help her and I am feeling bad about it. What does not help is that I took her on at a slightly higher rate than the rest of the staff and therefore increasing her hours would be an even greater expense. I have tried to explain this all to her and she appears to understand my worries but it does not stop me feeling uncomfortable about it all.

We are going to put on some events between now and Christmas to see if we can draw the custom in that way. With all our interest in the Paranormal we are going to have Psychic Nights once a month and Quiz Nights on a Sunday evening because that is always a very quiet evening. Bingo has also been scheduled into our weekly events. We always do very well Sunday lunchtime, generally selling out our roast dinners but we are still attracting a lot of ladies and older customers which is lovely but unfortunately none of these types of customers are drinkers and so the profits are still non-existent. We will also be having a couple of Disco Nights on Saturdays. Hopefully this mix of entertainment will bring in the customers.

The first couple of Psychic Nights were a huge success, Daniel our Medium comes by train and then I take him home once the evening is over. I always enjoy this drive because it gives me an opportunity to talk about the paranormal with someone other than Paul. I have explained to Daniel that I always feel as though I am missing something when I do my readings and I am not sure what I am doing wrong. He invites me to come to him for a reading at which time he will be able to talk me through how it all works. I am very excited by this opportunity and I cannot wait.

When the evening finally comes around that I am to visit Daniel for my reading I am so nervous. I needn't have been as it turns out because he is absolutely brilliant. My Nana came through and Daniel gave me so much information which he could not have known and proved that validation is what it is all about. He then stuns me by saying "Ok, your turn, now you can read me." My legs turned to jelly, this was a bit like Gordon Ramsey calmly telling me to make him dinner. But, never one to turn down a challenge I opened up. I got a Gentleman and we established that it was Daniel's uncle but I was not getting much beyond that. Daniel suddenly started firing questions at me which I was answering immediately and eventually I felt I had done a reasonable reading. When we were finished he asked me how I had known the answers to his questions. Had I heard the answers? Had I been given signs? I had to stop and think because at first I genuinely could not place how I had known the answers. "I seemed to just know." I told Daniel.

"And that is exactly what you have been feeling is missing." He explained. "Sometimes we just have to completely allow ourselves to open up and just 'feel' and this is how we get a lot of the answers, we just *know*."

Before I took on the pub I sang with a Ladies Choir but I gave it up when we started here as I knew I needed to devote all my time to making this work. I also gave up assisting with the Blue Falcons at this time as well. I have been contacted by the choir who have asked us to do a 'typically British' lunch for a choir who are visiting from France. I feel hugely honoured to have been asked to do this and I am pulling out all the stops. We have borrowed equipment to be able to do a Sunday roast carvery and I am also going to put on a salad based buffet for those who may not fancy a roast. We are lucky because although it is mid-September it is a lovely day and they will be able to use the garden as well as the pub. I have had to put up signs to say the pub is closed for a private event as we are expecting so many people. We have sectioned off half of the top of the bar to lay out all the Desserts. Lyn and I have been making home-made cakes and we have also bought in some other items which look delicious. All the staff are working today and it should be a really fun day.

All is going well so far, everyone seems to be enjoying the food and there have been no slip ups. Every time we do an event I wish we were getting more bookings for this type of thing as I am always so proud of what we can achieve. The boys also help and I love the way we all get on so well as a team. With the staff we are like one big family and it is wonderful. My worries about the health of the pubs trade pale into insignificance when I think about this. I may have said before that when my husband and I parted I did not feel like we were much of a family, the boys were out doing their own thing and I felt that family life was non-existent but the way they have all come together for this venture has filled my heart with joy. Today is a very happy day.

I am becoming increasingly concerned about Alec. Although he is a nice chap and always seems keen to please I know that he is taking stuff home from the kitchen. I think if he was that desperate and he had asked I might have said it was ok but then I wonder if that had happened would he have just taken advantage. He is still dreadful with his time keeping and I know I should deal with it but

I am useless when it comes to this type of thing. I am too much of a softy and I am sure many would say you cannot take that attitude as a business owner, so I am just letting it drift along and chastising myself daily for not dealing with it.

The money situation is reaching crisis point. It has almost all gone and I am dreading us having a hard winter for more than one reason. This is a very big, ancient building which is listed and therefore double glazing cannot be installed and I am worried about our heating bills over the winter. Also if it is really grotty weather, even more reason for the customers to not come.

Christmas is always a good time but then January and February can be dire. We have started getting parties booking for Christmas which is good news. We are not opening Christmas Day, we are just going to have a family Christmas together in the pub. Part of my reason for closing Christmas Day is our inability to put on a really fabulous dinner which would be expected on such a special day. We specialise in home cooked food and I have not got the confidence to lay on something exceptional without a fully trained chef. This makes me wonder if I am biting off my nose to spite my face by not hiring a chef. Maybe if we were known for fabulous food the customers would come and the outlay for an expensive chef would be worth it. However there are two fine dining establishments very close by and I had hoped that by going the home cooked route we would attract different custom.

I feel I need to be making some serious decisions before things really start to spiral out of control.

Sandra

I have been asked to go and do a reading for a couple of friends. I have known John and Pat for around 30 years and therefore I am a bit worried because I feel I know an awful lot about them and so providing information that I could not possibly have known, passed to me from the Spirit World may prove to be difficult. I am not sure how this is going to go. Neither of them have ever had a reading before and they decided it would be interesting to try it out.

When I arrive at their house I begin by explaining how it all works. It was John who particularly wanted the reading so I was going to concentrate on him. I told them that for some reason, which I have yet to understand, I hear a lot of names. I have realised that I do need to pass on these names as one could be relevant, although a lot of the time I feel it is just spirits passing through letting me know they are there.

I stood up to cross the room to sit next to John and as I did so I heard the name Sandra very clearly.

"Here we go." I laughed. "It has already started as I can hear the name Sandra." Pat gasped and clapped her hand to her mouth. "That is who John wanted to hear from!" She said, amazement making her eyes wide as she looked at me. I quickly sat down, not wishing to lose the contact I had obviously already made. I closed my eyes and concentrated on listening but also looking to see if I could see her. I became aware of a young girl, she was in a wheelchair. I voiced what I could see and John said that it was correct. I then began to experience pain in my head. John confirmed that she had had a brain tumour and was in a wheelchair before she died.

She gave me more information which all made sense to John and then suddenly I could see her standing in the middle of the room, she began to dance around smiling and laughing. I told John and Pat that she was letting us know that on the other side she was no longer suffering and was able to dance and play once more. As I watched her she stopped dancing and said to me that there was someone else here to see John and therefore she was just going to stay and listen. Before I could really register what was happening she began to run towards me, just as a toddler would who was intending to jump on your lap. Instinctively I took my hands out of my lap and quickly tucked them under my legs. I did it just in time as she launched herself on to me. It is very hard to describe exactly how this felt. The shock was incredible. It would never have occurred to me that this was possible. I was totally aware of her on my lap but there was no weight to her. It was almost as Daniel had described to me about knowing except that in this instance I could see her. She had tucked her legs under herself and was sitting facing Pat with her side leaning against my chest. I turned and looked at Pat, shock still vibrating through me.

"She is on your lap isn't she?" Whispered Pat, with exactly the same expression on her face as when I first said Sandra's name. I nodded, still barely able to believe it was happening.

"How did you know?" I asked.

"The way you moved." She replied. "Everything in your body language suggested that she had unexpectedly got on your lap."

John was staring at me. "You mean she is here? Sitting right here?" Poor John looked so shocked. He was sitting next to me and I think it was a bit close for comfort.

I took a deep breath and tried to calm myself. Sandra had told me someone else was wanting to speak to John. I explained this to them and waited to see what happened. I did not have to wait long because I immediately felt that there was a man standing right next to my legs. Quite why he felt he needed to be so near me I am not sure but I mentally acknowledged him and asked him how he had passed away. This is a good way to help identify who has come through if I am not getting their name. He showed me what looked like a cartoon, something you might see on Tom and Jerry. I could see a man's head but then half of the head appeared to break up into thousands of dots which then appeared to fly away. He showed me this over and over again and I could not make sense of it. In the end I explained to John and Pat that I did not understand what I was seeing so I was going to describe it to them. I explained and they both nodded in understanding. I generally ask whoever I am reading for not to tell me anything until the reading is over so that I cannot make any assumptions about the information I am receiving.

"Can we ask a question?" Asked Pat. "You can certainly try. I can only pass on what I hear or see but please make it as short and as quick as you can so that my thinking brain does not have time to start dwelling on it. I need to get the answer almost immediately you have asked the question or I will not be sure I was given the information rather than me thinking it."

"OK." Said Pat. "Where are you buried?" The answer came as fast as I thought it would but it made no sense to me. "He said, they left me there." I told them. Much to my surprise they both nodded as if it made perfect sense to them.

The man nodded to me and turned and disappeared. Sandra was still sitting on my lap. "He has gone." I told them. "But Sandra is still here."

"On your lap still." Laughed Pat. "You look as though you are scared to move."

I nodded. "It is odd, I have to admit, but not an unpleasant experience, I feel very energised and tingly as though our energies are combining. It is actually a lovely feeling."

"So would you like me to explain? Asked Pat.

"If you are happy to, I would love to hear." I replied. "I am quite confused and very surprised that in all the years I have known you I have never heard you mention Sandra."

"Sandra was John's cousin but they were neighbours so they were very close almost like brother and sister but they were only young when she died and therefore we never really talk about her because it was so long ago and the man was John's uncle but he never actually knew him as he died during the war. We went to the war graves in Tunisia to see his grave and whilst we were there I said to John 'I wonder if his body is here or if it is just a memorial stone.' So when you said *'they left me there'* that answered the question because he lost his life when he stood on a land mine. That is probably why he was trying to show you half of him disappearing. We did not think they could have found anything of him to bury after that sort of death and therefore he must have meant that he was left on the battlefield."

I was amazed to put it mildly. It just proves how the spirits can show things without actually explaining but what they show makes sense to those who are receiving the message. People have started asking me why the spirits do not just simply give full information if I can hear and see them. Believe me I wish I knew but to be honest the more I learn, the more questions without answers there seem to be. However, I know what I know and I am happy with that.

Pat and John told me how thrilled they were with how successful the reading had been and whilst we were talking I suddenly realised that Sandra had gone. She knew how happy we all were to have met her and did not feel the need to say goodbye. A couple of weeks after this I went up to the cemetery in Broomfield and was able to find her grave. It was just something I felt I wanted to do, I am not sure why but it was nice to find and acknowledge her.

Big Decisions

It is now November and I have to let Alec go. We do not have enough trade to warrant keeping him and he has not improved his timekeeping nor has he stopped taking items home without asking; so today I am going to tell him that I am letting him go and I am not looking forward to it at all. This is one part of being a business owner that I really do not like.

I ask Alec to come to my office and I sit him down to explain what is happening and my reasons for it. Surprisingly he is fine with it. He says he has been expecting it as he knows the business is struggling. He is so good about it that I begin to get upset and he ends up putting an arm round me and telling me not to worry as he knows he can find something else. I feel like such a fool... so unprofessional of me but as I have mentioned before we have been working together like one big family and he knows that I would not do this if I had any other choice. So that is that, he is going and I now have one less wage to try and find.

The money pot is empty and the takings are in no way near high enough to pay all the monthly outgoings. I have spoken to the Area Manager and he has said that the rent on the property which I pay monthly is going to be halved for 3 months to try and help me along. This is really good news but I know that unless things radically change it is still going to be a struggle. They keep reporting on the news that we are in a serious recession. There are also reports that the smoking ban has had a terrible effect on the pub trade. I am beginning to feel that I could not have taken on the pub at a worse time. Paul is still working which is an immense help as he pays for quite a lot and he has now offered to take out a loan to try and give the business a boost and to help us get through Christmas. Obviously all the food and drink has to be bought in before any events and his loan will help us to buy everything we need for the Christmas period.

I am worried about the amount of staff I have even without Alec I think there are too many of us and I keep going over and over it in my head. I need to be strong and act like a businesswoman. The burden of all this is really starting to weigh heavy.

Thank God Paul is with me. If I had taken on the business alone I do not know where I would be. He is such a support, not just with the financial help but he listens to my endless worrying, always offering a shoulder to cry on and supportive words of encouragement. He really is my rock. I worry that I am not giving him the love and devotion that I should as my mind seems to forever be on the pub but he tells me he enjoys the pub life as much as I do and is happy just the way things are. We try to see Paul's boys, Nathan and Daniel as regularly as we can, although juggling all the balls between Paul's shifts and when the boys are working and events in the pub it feels as though we do not see them often enough and this makes us sad. Hopefully when things improve we will be able to see more of them.

My sister Catherine, my Mum and I go on a Christmas shopping trip to Norwich every year, we stay overnight in a Bed and Breakfast which my Mum generously pays for. This has been a tradition for the three of us for years and this year is no exception. Pauline the landlady of the B & B greets us warmly after our long day of shopping in Norwich and we head off to our rooms to shower and get ready for our snuggly evening together. We eat dinner at lunch time whilst we are out and then have nibbles in our room in the evening. We all love this trip. We drag all our bags of shopping up to the rooms and gather in the room that Cath and I share. We spend the evening doing 'show and tell' with all our purchases before having tea in front of the telly. I have to admit my heart is not wholly in it this year, thoughts of the pub are never far from my mind but I try to push them away determined to enjoy a little 'me time' away from it all. I think the problem is I feel guilty, even though Mum pays for our trip I feel as though I should not be spending anything when my finances are so dire. But as usual Paul was a darling when I spoke to him about this before the trip and he told me that if I did not have some time away occasionally, I would send myself mad. Cath drove and I realised how tired I have become as I slept for most of the 2 hour journeys there and back.

It is the last week of November and it is time for the first Christmas party. Paul and I have spent the afternoon laying up and decorating the pub. Because of the size of the party we have moved the restaurant tables to the large centre bar and we have them laid out in lines. It looks beautiful. I am so thrilled. Paul and I work incredibly well together, I think it is because he accepts that I am a bit of a control freak and he therefore waits, so patiently bless him, while I tell him what I want and where I want it and off he goes to do as I have asked. I really could not love him more!

All the staff are in and ready, the boys are here too as it will be all hands on deck when it comes to taking the courses out. The atmosphere is brilliant as all the party guests arrive and begin to get seated. My excitement and nerves are through the roof but I know we will do a good job. The area usually used for the restaurant is clear and we have party dance music ready for when they have eaten. It should be a great night.

As we reach the time for coffee and tea I am in the kitchen with the staff and the boys. "I just want to thank you all." I say as we all prepare for the final stage of the evening. "Tonight has been a massive success and I particularly want to thank Lyn for all her brilliant work with tonight's menu and not just tonight; In the nine months that we have been in the pub we have never had a meal sent back to the kitchen including this evening and I think that is an absolutely wonderful thing to be able to say about a food establishment. I am so proud of everyone, those that were cooking and sending out the food, all of you behind the bar and the food servers, you all did brilliantly, I honestly could not be more proud!" We all gave ourselves a little round of applause with lots of happy satisfied smiles and then as the music started up for the dancing, the bar staff returned to carry on serving drinks while the rest of us set about the Mammoth task of clearing up.

I am back in my little office above the pub with paperwork spread out in front of me. The joy and excitement of the first Christmas party have rapidly faded away. I have to face reality and let one of the members of staff go. Lyn's husband died a few years ago and I know that the financial difficulty would be dreadful for her. I also am aware of how much she loves it here, it is like her second home and she is the most loyal, devoted member of staff I could ever hope for. This added to the fact that she is the main cook and I absolutely could not do without her means that she cannot be considered. Pam and Lyn are both coming up for 60. If I let either of them go I am unsure they will be able to get another job and therefore Pam cannot be considered either. Amy only does a few hours on occasional evenings and therefore it would not be much of a saving to let her go. That brings me back to Jo and the very thought of it makes my heart hurt.

She is brilliant with the customers and so good at her job that I am totally confident that she will not have any trouble finding another job but I know how this is going to make her feel and I can barely stand the thought of having to tell her but I have absolutely no choice and having made the decision I feel I should go to her home to tell her. I do not want to tell her here. I hope that she understands. Paul is off today and he is manning the bar, so I tell him where I am going. He takes me in his arms and hugs me tight. "Good luck Sweetheart," he whispers, "I know how hard this is going to be for both of you."

I reach Jo's front door and my legs are shaking so badly that for a moment I think I am actually going to collapse. As she opens the door and sees me standing there her face says it all. She steps aside to let me in. "I am so sorry Jo, I just do not know what else to do. It is a dreadful time to do this with Christmas coming but I really cannot afford to carry on. With your wages being the highest of all the staff by letting you go I am making the biggest saving." I could hear myself saying the words and they sounded so hollow and then to my fury I started to cry. Crying is my worst weakness and it catches me unaware at the most awful of times. She should be the one crying. I have just told her, right before Christmas that she has lost her job, I would completely understand if she flew off the handle at me and threw me out of the house but instead she takes me in her arms and tells me it is fine, that she understands, having been there from day one and seeing how the business is not really taking off she had been expecting it. She almost echoes what Alec had said. Hearing those words does not make it any easier and I leave with my head hanging in shame. I feel as though I have let her down so badly but I could see no way out.

Breakfast

T he rest of the Christmas parties were a huge success and December as expected was our best month so far. We had a fabulous New Year's Eve party but as we enter January the dread and fear are never far from my mind, it is like a crushing feeling that sits in my chest and my mind races trying to find answers as to how we can bring about a change.

Christopher is out of work and although he is a huge help in the pub I am trying to find a way to increase our takings and find him more to do so I come up with the idea of breakfasts. He has a friend who is also not working and I sit them down and suggest my plan to them. I explain that if they are willing to be in the pub by 6.30am to open and have the kitchen ready for 7.00am then they are both more than capable of running breakfasts together. They both seem very interested and I can tell from the way that they look at each other that they are excited at being given this opportunity. I tell them that I will do two days a week to give them a break. So it is decided, we will start in a week's time.

As we are so close to the A12 I am hoping that the early morning travellers might be tempted in by this offer. I purchase another banner advertising the breakfasts and I also put an ad in the local magazine. Along the A12 there is a bridge that is no longer in operation. They closed off that country lane when the new road was built so half the bridge is right on the side of the road. I have a big metal sign made and Paul and I go and attach it to the bridge. It looks fantastic from the road, it tells the drivers that they can get breakfasts just off of the next slip road. We also get permission from the house at the top of the slip road to have a sign on their wall directing customers to the pub. I am so pleased with the advertising and I have high hopes for our breakfast trade. The more people that come through the door and enjoy the experience of visiting our pub, the more likely they are to come back at other times of the day.

Although worry is my constant companion I am still desperately happy to be where we are. Ever the optimist, I am sure it will turn around and we will have many, many wonderful years here. Friends and family are being so supportive. Mum and Dad come once a week for lunch and friends are often unexpectedly popping in. I have two very good friends in the village, Sandra and Alayne, we were at school together and it is wonderful to still be in touch. Alayne's parents come in once a week. Maureen, Alayne's Mum is a great fan of our Beef Stew and her Dad always has an Omelette. This evening my friend Nicola and her sister have been in. Nicola was a huge support to me when I was on my own and is a dear friend. She does amuse me, she always gets very excited to be having dinner in the pub as she loves our Steak Pie.

It is times like this that make me so happy to be here, I love to entertain and being the host in a pub ticks so many boxes for me.

Another of my happy times, strangely, is when I am cleaning the pub in the mornings. I have music playing to keep me company and I take pride in keeping the appearance to a high standard and simply enjoying what I have created. Occasionally Phoebe will appear and dance along with me, it always makes me feel like I am glowing when she shows herself to me and her enthusiasm for the dancing leaves me breathless and exhilarated. I am aware that she is around whenever I do a reading or open up for some reason, I know that she is there supporting me. It seems odd to suggest that young child is helping me but the world of spirit is on a level which we will never understand. I see her and feel her as a child but I know there is much more to her than that. When she is not dancing with me, for instance if I am doing a reading or just having a bit of quiet time and I become aware of her I always sense her behind my right shoulder.

As I expected January is proving to be the quietest month so far. It is cold and I am having to try to keep the pub as warm as I can. There is nothing worse than sitting in a cold pub. I cannot think of anything more unwelcoming.

Chris and Bradley are doing a few breakfasts but yet again it is nothing like I had hoped for but we have to press on with it, we need word of mouth to start to spread to bring in the trade.

The Keys

January is nearly over and I have been running the bar on my own this evening. As it has been so quiet since Christmas we only need one in the kitchen and one on the bar. The kitchen closes at 9pm and Lyn has cleaned down and gone home. Paul is on nights and the boys are all out for the evening. I have just finished cleaning down the bar and it is time to lock up. I lock the side garden entrance first and then the main front doors, I do the kitchen door last. This is the door that all the family and staff use as the entrance to get in. Once all the doors are locked I do a full sweep of the pub, starting in the lobby at the front of the pub, into the toilets, coffee lounge, main bar and restaurant and finally the toilet at the garden entrance. Once I have fully checked those areas I go down the passage to the cellar and check that is clear, make sure the outer cellar doors are locked and then make one final check of the kitchen. When all of this is done I hang the big bunch of keys on the board in the little lobby area between the kitchen and the bar and head upstairs with the tills. This is a habit I have developed ever since we moved in. If Paul is home we do it between us but when I am the only one in the whole building I do it alone. After cashing up the tills I then head up to my office to check them. Once this is done and I am satisfied that everything tallies I put them away ready with the right cash to start the day tomorrow. It is easier to do it this way than setting the tills up in the morning.

This evening the takings are terrible and I sit at my desk gazing into space, too tired to really think properly about how things are going, I just seem to go over the same thoughts time and time again.

Eventually I decide there is no point sitting here I might as well get to bed where I can snuggle up and watch a bit of telly before calling Paul to wish him goodnight.

Popping down the stairs to get myself a drink of squash and turn off all the lights for the night I enter the lobby and movement catches my eye, something is moving on the key board. The bunch of keys that I use to lock up everywhere is swinging from side to side. If you were looking at a clock face I would say they were swinging from twenty past the hour to twenty to the hour. How on earth are they still moving? I have been upstairs for a good half hour and no one else is in the building. For some strange reason this sort of thing never worries me. I think having grown up with odd experiences it is something I am used to. Leaning my shoulder on the wall by the stairs I settle down to watch. Back and forth they rock. I pride myself in always looking for a scientific reason before I jump to the paranormal explanation and therefore I begin looking around to see if I can detect a draught that might be blowing them but even as I start to do this I realise that there are other smaller bunches of keys some with little card tags attached to them and not one of them is moving. If it was a draught there would be at least some other movement. I then wonder if it is vibration of some description but again the same applied, they are the only bunch moving. The whole time I stand considering this they continue to move. They are moving as a solid item, they are not jingling, it is as if someone has hold of them as a bunch and is just moving them from side to side. The hairs on my neck begin to stand on end. This is paranormal.

I move to the dead centre of the lobby area, the audio equipment is behind me and I am facing the stairs. To my left is the door to the pub and my right the doors to the passage and the kitchen. The keys are still moving and I feel as though time is standing still. Maybe it is my little old lady that I have seen here and other members of staff have heard. Maybe she wants to contact me for some reason. I decide to 'open up' and let her speak to me. As I begin to open my mind I sense a huge presence. Shock shoots through me, this is not my little lady! It is something much more powerful. It is a male and he has massive energy. I can feel him circling me. The only way I can really describe it, is to say it is like a huge black cape coming from above me but beginning to swirl around me. With absolute certainty I know that his intention is to somehow merge with me, I know it is his way of making contact but I am scared. I have never encountered anything like this and I am not prepared to allow it to happen, certainly not whilst I am alone.

I cry out in panic. "No!" And he has gone. As soon as I shouted it was as if the spell had been broken and he left. I know in my very soul that he had not meant any harm but I had simply not got the courage to face whatever he was here for whilst I was alone. I look over at the keys and see that the bunch has stopped moving completely.

My entire body is shaking: I quickly get my drink, close all the doors around me, turn off the lights and head upstairs. I cannot wait to speak to Paul and find out what he thinks of this amazing experience.

Once I am in bed I call Paul. He listens in silence while I explain what happened this evening. "Are you ok?" He asks. Bless him, always worried about me.

"I am fine." I assure him. "Just fascinated to be honest as I really cannot think what was going on or why I felt he was trying to somehow merge with me rather than just speaking to me."

Paul sighed. "I must admit I have no idea either, I have never heard of anything like that. Especially as you say you did not feel threatened but just did not want to deal with it alone. Maybe it would be worth speaking to Daniel to ask him if he has any ideas."

"That sounds like a good plan." I agreed. "I certainly will not be going straight to sleep, I am going to watch a bit of telly as I feel too excited to sleep at the moment."

We said our goodnights and I settled down, my life just seems to get stranger by the day.

Susie and Don are regulars who come in at least once a week for their dinner after work. On this particular evening whilst they were eating Susie spotted a poster advertising the psychic event. "Shall we get tickets to watch?" Susie was saying to Don as I cleared their plates.

"It is a load of rubbish." Don stated, looking a little peeved.

"He really is good." I told him as I winked at Susie. "Why don't you stay? It is a horrible winter evening, what else would you be doing instead?"

"Watching something decent on the telly." Grumbled Don who knew he was going to have to give in.

Half an hour later the evening's crowd had assembled. Much to my amusement I spotted that Susie had got front row seats and Don was looking decidedly uncomfortable.

Daniel started by explaining to all those who had never been to an evening of this type before how it would all work and the excitement amongst the audience was palpable.

Two very successful readings had been given and it was almost time for the interval. Suddenly Daniel turned and looked straight at Don. "I have a man here for you." Don shook his head and quite honestly I thought he was going to run from the room. "It isn't for me, I don't believe in all this stuff, I am just here with my wife." Daniel shrugged with a little laugh. "It is not to do with what you believe, if someone on the other side wishes to communicate with you via me I am afraid there is nothing we can do to stop them." Daniel looked up towards the ceiling, clearly concentrating on what he was being told. "This is your brother, he has been gone some time but is thrilled to be able to contact you." Don looked uncomfortable and did not say anything. Daniel carried on regardless, he began giving him information and Don was looking more and more astounded. Daniel held up his right hand.

"My little finger is missing." Shock flooded Dons face and his eyes filled with tears. "My brother did not have his little finger on his right hand, he lost it in an accident." Susie began to stroke his back in an attempt to offer a little comfort. Daniel continued to give some more information and then said that he would leave it there. He offered Don his brother's love and ended the first session.

Everyone was up and talking at once. Amy and Paul went behind the bar to arrange drinks and coffees for those who wanted them. Don and Susie had gone out into the garden, I followed them out to find a very embarrassed Don still shedding some tears. "I cannot believe it." He whispered as I walked up to them. "He could not have known about my Brother, there is absolutely no way he could have known and yet he was able to tell me so much." I knew they were happy tears and I gave his arm a little squeeze. There was nothing I needed to say. This type of experience blows the mind a little, especially when you have entered into it a total non-believer.

The evening was over and I was driving Daniel home. "I have a question for you." I said, breaking the companionable silence. "Well, not so much a question, it is more that I want your opinion on something which happened recently." I explained the story of the keys. I told him in minute detail so that I was sure he understood fully what had happened.

"The fact that he used the keys to attract your attention suggests to me that it is probably your Gatekeeper trying to let you know he is around you." Daniel explained.

"Ok, but what do you mean by my Gatekeeper?" I asked.

"He is your strongest guide. He will be the one who takes care of you. All your guides protect you and help you but he will be by far the most important, most powerful of your guides. We are all supposed to have one, they keep everything in order. I think it is important that you try to meet him but make it on your terms.

He tried to introduce himself to you but I do not think he fully appreciated how overwhelming it would be for you. When you have a quiet moment, when you can take yourself to a calm state of mind you can call him to you. If it makes you more comfortable have Paul with you to keep an eye on you to ensure that no harm comes to you but I can assure you it won't. The very fact that he left as soon as you said no, shows that he respects your wishes."

"So what do I do exactly"? I asked.

"Make it a time when you know that you will not be interrupted. Sit quietly and try to clear your mind. Just completely relax, open up and wait and see what happens. He will know you are calling for him and he will come. Incidentally I am saying him because you felt that the presence was male but it could just as easily be a woman."

"Thank you Daniel." I said as we pulled into his driveway. "Both for this evening and for all your advice. I really do appreciate it."

Having explained to Paul what Daniel had suggested we were both keen to take it further. Trade is still very low so we decided this evening to close at 10pm. We had had nobody through the door since 9pm and the pub was now empty. The boys were all out so we had the building to ourselves.

"Let's sit in the bar." I suggested. We got ourselves soft drinks and sat on barstools at the bar.

"Would you like me to help you get to a quiet place?" Asked Paul.

"That would be lovely, just keep an eye on me please, I am really nervous."

Paul smiled. "You will be fine. I know you will. As Daniel said, whoever this is wants to meet you and would not do anything to scare or hurt you."

"Close your eyes Sweetheart and try to relax as much as you can." I have always loved listening to Paul's voice so I instantly felt my body begin to allow all the tension to drain away. "I want you to picture yourself in a garden, there is no one else around and it is so quiet. The only sounds you can hear are birdsong. As you begin to walk through the garden you are surrounded as far you can see on all sides by beautiful red flowers. Follow the path and concentrate on allowing your body to relax as you look at the flowers and listen to the birds singing. Now as you walk you will notice that the flowers have now become a lovely orange colour, you are surrounded by orange. Feel all the tension washing away from your body. Keep walking and you will see that the flowers are now yellow, all around you as far as you can see. The birdsong is becoming a little quieter and you are feeling incredibly relaxed. Now look around, all of the flowers are white. I want you to stop walking and just stand for a moment and see what you can see."

My body was tingling, I had followed Paul's instructions and I felt as though I were floating on air. As I looked at the white flowers they began to change, they slowly were disappearing and I realised I was standing in a room but this room had no windows or doors. Everything was white, the floor, ceiling and walls. I almost felt as though I was standing inside a white box although I knew it was a room and I felt completely safe and relaxed. As I stood there I became aware of a man in front of me. He seemed to slowly appear from the feet upwards. He was incredibly tall. He was balding but had some mousey blonde hair, he had a beard and was wearing long white robes.

He smiled but did not speak. "Are you a Shepherd?" I asked. He laughed, a very deep low voiced laugh. "No, Judith, I am not a Shepherd. I am a Shaman. I am your main spirit guide as a Shaman cannot have anything less than another Shaman to look over them." I stared at him trying to make sense of this statement.

"So you are saying that I am a Shaman?" He nodded.

"You have many lessons to learn and you will follow a path to learn these lessons as you go. I will be with you as well as your other guides, some you are already aware of and some you have yet to meet. My name is Brian and it has been a pleasure to finally meet you."

Before I could think of what else to ask him, he slowly disappeared in much the same way as he had appeared.

I opened my eyes. Paul was staring at me expectantly. I smiled and leant into him. "Just give me a moment, I need to process what just happened." Paul put his arm round me and I could feel the beating of his heart. His breathing was slow and rhythmic and for that moment all thoughts of the pub left my mind. I was completely content and deeply happy.

After a moment or two I sat back up. "Well that was amazing, there are no other words to describe it. I will try to tell you exactly what happened and how it felt."

To say that Paul was shocked would be an under-statement. "I have tremendous faith in your gifts darling but I honestly was not sure what would happen there. I never in my wildest dreams would have imagined that he would come and actually have a conversation with you. So I was right, you are a Shaman." I lowered my head in embarrassment not wanting to face what I had been told.

"It really is ok Sweetheart, how many times do I have to tell you that I feel you have some really special gifts. But I do find it quite sweet that you are so loath to accept all this. You just have to ride with it. As Brian said you are on a path and learning lessons there is no more that you can do than to allow it to happen."

We finished our drinks and headed off upstairs. I feel as though it may take me a little time to get to sleep tonight. My mind is spinning with it all.

Shifting Sands

Paul and I are in the kitchen and Amy is on the bar, we have done very little food tonight so we are cleaning down. February has arrived with talk of snow and my misery is growing. I have decided to take out a loan. The loan that Paul took out has gone. I have never been in debt like this before and it worries the life out of me. Of course everyone has a certain amount of debt. When I was married we had our Mortgage and credit cards but we never let the debt get too high on the cards, we always paid them off as soon as we could but being in a business like this is a whole other level. Every bill is so much higher than that of a domestic bill. I find myself dealing with such large figures. Simply putting an order in to the Brewery each week costs a fortune and it pains me dreadfully when we have to throw away real ale. Matthew and I are very diligent when it comes to cleaning the pipes and I pride myself in the quality of my real ale. Those that drink it often comment on what a good pint it is. I often wonder if other landlords allow their beer to go slightly out of date but I could not bring myself to do that. As I have stated before I am a stickler for doing everything by the book which means that when the beer reaches it date I have to tip the rest of the barrel away and with trade being what it is I sometimes have to tip away at least half a barrel if not more. I feel as though I am watching money go down the drain.

"I am going to take out a loan." I say to Paul as we work.

He turns and stares at me. "Why are you going to borrow more money? You have the money I got for you before Christmas."

"It has gone." I reply miserably.

He gasps. "How can it have gone? It was a fortune." He frowns in anger and confusion. The way he looked at me tore at my heart. I did not want him to feel I was failing and yet I was certain I was. I just simply could not seem to encourage more trade. Tears threatened. Usually when he sees something has upset me he comes straight to me to offer support and a shoulder to cry on. But this time he just continued to stare at me. I felt as though he was accusing me. What could he possibly think I had done with the money? I am in the pub 24/7, I have never been a girly girl. I do not wear make-up, I am not one for clothes, bags or shoes. Any money I have ever spent over the years has either been on the children or my business and I thought he understood that.

"It was a lot of money Paul but I cannot tell you how much it costs to keep this place afloat, the rent, the wages, the food and drink. Add to that all the usual like electricity, gas, music licence, pest control, the waste collection, it goes on and on and with such pitiful takings we are continually falling short."

"I thought the brewery gave you three months half rent?"

"They did but it is still a fortune, I honestly cannot tell you how much everything costs". The silence that follows is deafening. For the first time since we had met I felt that he was really cross with me and I could see no way to make it better. With his head down he muttered "I am going to let Amy go home, you can go up and have a rest". He walked away, no hug, no kiss. I felt weak with sadness as I went up the stairs to have a bath. I know deep down he is not angry with me, he is scared, we are finding ourselves in a situation neither of us had envisaged and we simply do not know how to deal with it.

Paul and I have been together two years now. I cannot believe how much we have been through in such a short space of time but what I have learnt of him, is to not carry on talking. He needs time to process what I have just told him.

About an hour later he comes into the bedroom. "I have put the tills away." He tells me as he walks through the door. "I cashed them up but I have not prepared them for the morning."

"That's fine, thank you, I will do them tomorrow." I reply smiling at him gently.

"Are you ok?" I ask. He nods ruefully as he perches on the end of the bed.

"Yea, I am alright, it just came as a bit of a shock when you said about the loan. I had not really considered that the money I got for us would be gone already. Frightening times eh Sweetheart?"

I nodded sadly. "Indeed they are. Get yourself ready for bed, I think we could both do with a cuddle."

The bank agreed the loan. I felt so ashamed talking to them but they were actually really good about it; acknowledging how difficult the pub trade was at the moment and they assured me I was not alone in having to reach out for help. Going into the pub in a blaze of glory was fast disappearing and my high hopes for a long and bright future in this trade were beginning to fade. However I could not let these thoughts put me down. I was still taking tremendous pride in looking after the place. I love the building so much. On the days that Phoebe joins me as I am cleaning her presence boosts me. One thing I do know about myself is that I am a fighter, if anything puts me down I will always shake myself off, dust myself down and carry on. And so with the new injection of money I can relax slightly and put all my efforts into running the business with everything I have got.

Synchronicity

I have two ladies coming this evening. They heard about me through a friend and want readings and as I have not done any for a while it will be quite nice to have a practice.

When they arrived we tucked ourselves away at the back of the lounge area. The readings for both ladies have been going well, one of them has her daughter with her, she must be in her early twenties and she has just come along to see what would happen. I began to see a man, he was very agitated and I was having trouble understanding what he wanted. He made me feel that there was a lot of confusion in his mind. He was also showing me that there had been violence although he made it clear that this was not intentional. I told the ladies that I felt he was trying to tell me that this was as a result of Dementia and that he was not responsible for his actions. I was able to describe how the gentleman looked. After a while the young lady said that she felt that this was her boyfriend's Grandfather but that he was still alive. I have heard that there have been cases noted where someone has made contact whilst in a deep coma, almost as if their spirit is able to communicate because of their mental state. I wondered if this could also apply to someone in the later stages of Dementia.

"Perhaps you could let your boyfriend know that this happened tonight. I really do not know what to say other than that maybe he should know." The ladies thanked me and asked if I wanted any money for the reading but I refused. I feel quite strongly that I should not charge for what I am doing as it is a gift and I do not want to benefit from it.

The following day was freezing and the forecast predicted snow. Sure enough just after lunch the snow started and was settling fast and by the evening it was quite deep on the ground. I had told the staff that we would man the pub ourselves this evening rather than dragging them out in such horrid weather. As I suspected we did not have anyone in at all and by 8pm I was considering closing. Paul and I cleaned down the bar and Paul went up to watch telly. Just as I was about to start locking up a young man came rushing through the door.

"Are you the lady that does the readings?" He asked. He seemed quite distressed and I went round the bar to him.

"Yes, I am, are you ok?" I asked as I steered him towards a table.

"You had my girlfriend here last night. You told her you thought my Grandad was talking to you."

"Yes." I replied. "I have never experienced that before so I am not sure what was happening when your girlfriend said he was still alive." I went back to the bar and got us both a lemonade. When I sat down beside him I asked again if he was ok.   "Can you try to talk to him for me? He asked. "He does not know we are there most of the time, it is so hard seeing him like that." I touched his hand in an attempt to calm him. "I can certainly try, let me just explain how it works so that you understand what I am doing and then we can see what we can do."

Once we were both settled and ready to start I closed my eyes. I heard a lady speaking to me in a calm, soothing voice. She told me she was the young man's Grandmother.

"I have your Nana here, she has a lovely voice, so calming. I opened my eyes to look at him and he was staring at me. I began passing on information to him and he looked more and more stunned. Sometimes when doing a reading I find it easier to stare at a blank surface, it helps me to see with my mind's eye. I was staring at the polished table top trying to see anything or hear what else she had to say to me.   "She is referring to you as her Little Chicken." I said without looking at him. He made a slight noise and I sensed that he had begun to cry. I closed my eyes for a second and as I opened them right in the centre of the table was a ladybird but the strange thing was (as if appearing in the middle of winter wasn't strange enough) it was not the usual red with black spots it was beige with lines on it and the only way I could truly describe it was that it made me think of the Burberry check pattern. It was very odd indeed. What I did next was also strange. Instead of exclaiming at the sudden appearance of this Ladybird I simply put out my hand towards it and with one finger I pointed, almost touching the tiny creature. The young man gasped and his initial quiet tears turned to sobs. I put my hand on his back and rubbed gently trying to calm him and offering comfort at the same time.

Eventually he managed to bring himself under control.

"My Nana used to call me her 'little Chicken' and when you said that I was so shocked but I still could not really believe that you were talking to her, so in my mind I asked her to give me a sign and straight away that ladybird appeared and you pointed to it, almost as if it was her pointing at it to say 'here you are' because what on earth would a Ladybird be doing around at this time of year?" He looked at me with wonder on his face. "It is my Nana and I think it was her talking to you last night, she showed you my Grandad to make me come here. My girlfriend did not know my Nana so there would have been no point my Nana coming through last night because my girlfriend would have not known who she was, let alone know she was connected to me. I honestly cannot believe it!"

"They call it Synchronicity." I said. "It is when a series of events occur which seem coincidental but lead to a pre-destined outcome." In other words it was deliberate on the part of your Nana. She knew I was seeing your girlfriend and she used that moment to contact you. The spirits never cease to amaze me in their ability to achieve things they need to happen."

Little did I realise that there was far more to this than I originally thought. Once the young man got over his initial shock and his Nana had left we began chatting. He completely opened up to me. I think it helped that I was a stranger and he had come to trust me through the guidance of his Nana. It transpired that he was in a really unhappy state to the point of having been considering taking his own life. We talked and talked until he felt it was time to leave. He had been with me for over two hours and I really felt that the visit from his Nana and our long conversation had helped him to feel much better. The energy I was picking up from him now was much stronger and more positive.

"Let me give you some money." He said putting his hand in his pocket to find his wallet.

"No." I replied. "I really do not want you to give me anything. Knowing how much I have been able to help you is payment enough for me. I have only been doing this a short while and seeing how much better you feel, tells me that I am using my gift in the correct way but I should not be doing it for money." He stood looking at me for a moment and then reached out for a hug.

"I really cannot thank you enough." He said as he turned to leave. I sat back down suddenly feeling drained from the events of the last couple of hours. As he approached the bar he leant over it then turned and gave me a wave as he went out of the door. I went over to the bar to see why he had leant over there and laying on the bar was a £20 note. I picked it up and walked back to where we had been sitting. The Ladybird was still there just sitting in the middle of the table. I gently picked it up and placed it on one of the plants in the corner of the bar.

As I moved around the pub locking up I began wondering about the fact that he had left the money. He clearly felt he should pay for what he considered to have been a service. Just because I was happy to do it for people did not mean that they would come. Maybe this was a lesson for me. It is all very well just saying I will not charge but that being the case, are people not going to want to come as they do not like to ask for a favour? Maybe money should exchange hands. What was the saying that the old fortune tellers used to say? 'Cross my palm with Silver,' maybe there was a reason for that. I definitely need to give this more thought.

I suddenly realised that Paul had not been down to check why it had taken me so long to come upstairs but the poor man is probably fast asleep in front of the television. It cannot be easy for him helping me in the pub and holding down a full time job. Time for bed I think.

We are into March. We have been here a year now and not one month has passed where we have made a profit. Not even December which to me is shocking. Christmas should be the best time of year. I have heard tell that some businesses run for the full year almost entirely living off of their Christmas takings. I keep hearing references on the news about the recession. Honestly! Not only did we take on a pub just after they introduced the smoking ban which is described as having had a terrible effect on the pub trade but now we are in a recession as well. I really hope the tide starts turning soon or I feel we are doomed.

The advertising for us being an 'event venue' brought in a few parties which as always were massive successes but still the general day to day trade is so slow.

Chris and Brad are pushing on with the breakfasts. When they first started Paul and I got up early one morning and they did breakfast for us, partly because I wanted to check that they were doing a good job and I was thrilled with the way they worked as a team and the breakfast was really good. However it has been a couple of months now and early morning trade is not good. I am beginning to wonder if we should call time on the breakfast idea. What has not helped is I have had a letter from the council. Someone has reported us for putting up a sign on the little brick bridge by the A12 and they have told us we must remove it immediately or face a fine. I feel so sad that someone out there felt they should report us but maybe I should have sought permission to put it up, it really did not occur to me. So Paul and I are going out this morning to take it down. I have been trying to think where else we could put it but my heart really is not in it. I think I know that it is time to stop the breakfasts I am just trying to work out how to break it to Chris and Brad, they have tried so hard. It feels like another body blow.

As it turned out they took it well. They are both sensible enough to know that it was not generating enough trade for us to carry on and they both seemed glad to get back to normal days. Time for them to look for jobs.

The pressure is starting to build

A s we drift into May I am finding I love the early mornings. Even though we do not go to bed until late I have always been an early riser and I take my breakfast out into the garden to have a few minutes quiet before the start of the day. I love it out here, May is such a beautiful month and so much is in bloom. I also sit out here late on a Sunday afternoon and have my roast dinner when the last of the customers have gone. If Paul is off he joins me and it is the only time at the moment that we really seem to get some time together alone.

When I sit out here in the mornings I try to forget everything for a while and just enjoy being amongst the flowers. I appreciate the sun on me and try to remind myself how lucky we are to live in such a lovely old building with all our strange ghosts and how fortunate we are to have this beautiful garden.

It is now two years since Maddie went missing. They have not found her and my desperate feeling of wanting to help has not lessened. So this morning I called the Leicestershire Police Headquarters to try to speak to someone about it. I was put through to a very nice police officer and I explained to him that I felt that if I could describe exactly what I saw to an artist who could do an impression of the area, maybe someone local might recognise it. He was very understanding about how I was feeling but he assured me that they would have had my information in Portugal and if anyone had wanted to know more I would have been contacted. Something that did shock me though was that he said to me not to go to Portugal to try to find where I believed where she was buried. He told me that 'lots of psychics' had been going out there and getting into a lot of trouble for digging up where they thought she was buried. To my mind this was even more reason to try to follow up on psychic information. Did they not think it strange if this was happening? It also comforted me to know that I was not the only one who felt this way but I had to accept I could do no more.

This morning whilst hoovering the pub, it was going through my head how taking out loans was all very well but then you simply have to add the monthly payments to the ever growing list of bills that need paying each month. My previous business was a small recruitment agency and I did all the paperwork myself including the wages for the girls and my own tax returns but since I have been in the pub I have used a firm of Accountants to do the wages and they will be doing my tax return for me this year. I am sure that will make very miserable reading. I supply them with all the paperwork they need each month so it should not be too difficult to put together.

The hoover seems to be getting heavier and heavier as I consider how this is all going to pan out. But I know I cannot let it beat me. We are still getting such lovely comments about our food. Sundays are still very successful with our roast dinners. Before we took over the pub several friends suggested to me that we make it a carvery as there is not one in the area. I am beginning to wonder if that would have been a good idea but it seems too late now to consider changing. I could not afford to buy all the equipment we would need now anyway. It has reached the point where I am running out of ideas. Any changes that I might consider are out of the question with there being no money to spend.

Jo has been in a couple of times with her Mum for a drink and it has been lovely to catch up with her. She was telling me today that she and her boyfriend Rich are thinking of taking on their own pub. She is so excited which I can completely understand but part of me wants to warn her against it but then I realise that it is not my place and every business is different. She could have far more success than me. I wish her all the luck in the world and cannot help feeling a little envious of the excitement she is feeling. Is it really only just over a year since I had those very same feelings? How quickly things can change.

I seem to be in my own head a lot lately, all I do is think. Today I have been thinking about friends and family. My two brothers and my sister have been supportive and popped in occasionally as have many of my friends but I rarely socialise anymore, I have had invites recently but I keep turning them down stating that I am too busy in the pub. The truth is I am finding it difficult facing people and admitting to them, when they ask, that we are struggling. I am an honest person so would not make up false tales of how well it is going and I find it so hard voicing the pain I am in. Paul has tried to encourage me to go out occasionally. He feels that it is doing me harm staying so close to home all the time but it is easier for me. It is a bit like hiding but I feel safe here and if I am here working then I feel I am doing everything I can to make this venture work. We do pop to Cambridge occasionally for Paul to catch up with his two sons. They have both visited the pub which has been lovely and Paul's brothers and sisters came at the beginning of March for a meal. They gather each year at this time to have a meal to remember their Mum. Paul's sister was here from America and it was lovely to meet her too.

The only person who I am not being entirely truthful with is our Area Manager, he pops in from time to time to see how we are doing and I put on my happy, smiling face and tell him we are fine. I suspect however that he would know that this is not entirely true from my purchasing levels on the drink. They drop a little further each month as I try to cut out as much as I can in order to buy the drink that is selling well.

On top of not seeing much of family and friends I feel as though Paul and I are drifting apart. As my mood is dropping I am aware that the awful green dragon that lives in my head is beginning to show itself. I have always hated the fact that I have a jealous streak. I try to do my very best to contain it because I know it is irrational but as with any personality trait if it is how you are then it takes a certain amount of willpower to keep it in check. If I could change one aspect of my personality it would definitely be to get rid of my jealousy. I tell myself not to be daft when I feel it coming over me but if I am down anyway it manages to have free reign over my feelings.

Just lately I feel as though Paul cannot wait to get to work. I would imagine most people would say they were not surprised to hear this. It must be a relief to get away from the pressures of pub life and also of course to be able to mix with other people. I think part of the reason I feel so bad is that I cannot escape. The pressure is always there and I feel I am in a Catch 22 situation. I do not want to go out and socialise but at the same time I am jealous that Paul gets to walk away. I can see how bad this sounds. I know I made my bed and I should lie in it but I cannot help how I feel and I know that I am taking it out on him. That being the case, no wonder he cannot wait to get to work to get away from me for a while. Because of this we do keep sniping at each other and that makes me feel so sad.

When we first moved into the pub Paul used to comment on how much he loved working in the kitchen with me and what a great team we were but just lately even this does not seem to be the case. I know it is my fault, I get impatient with him and moan if he does not do something exactly as I would have done it. It is a vicious circle. I know when I do it I have hurt him and I try to make up for it later and he forgives me and then days later I do it all over again. I feel so bad for him. He must wonder at times what an earth he has got himself into.

I find myself asking him about who he works with; wondering if his eagerness to get to work is because of another female and as you can imagine this infuriates him. He knows why I am asking. I have told him that I can be jealous but generally I am able to keep it in check but unfortunately having admitted this trait to him he is now worried every time I start asking questions.

I twist myself into tight knots worrying about this on top of everything else. I have to admit if I was in Paul's shoes I would be seriously considering going back to Cambridge as fast as my car could take me.

Don't get me wrong, there are plenty of good times. I love to work in the kitchen with Lyn, she really brightens my day, she is so down to earth and capable and she makes me feel safe. Also of course with all three boys and their partners being here a lot of the time there is always plenty of activity to keep me amused. I love to mix with the customers when I am helping out on the bar or serving in the restaurant and our weekly evening entertainment is still going strong so I have much to be thankful for. There is still a spark of hope inside me that the fortunes of the pub will change and that a brighter future lays ahead

I have resolved to be more considerate of Paul. No matter how I am feeling I must try to not let it show too much. I cannot imagine how it must feel having to come home to my worries and woes and unfortunately it is always him who has to listen as I really would not want to burden anyone else with my concerns. I have several friends and members of my family who I know would be mortified to hear me say this. I know that they would want me to talk to them about how I am feeling but unfortunately I can't. I feel such a fool for being so sure I could do this. My pride is keeping me from admitting to anyone just how bad our situation is.

My Brother Robert popped in this evening, he regularly pops in for a pint and sometimes if I am on the bar he offers to help out so that I can have a rest.

Tonight was different though. He looked a little sheepish and I knew that he had something to say. He chatted away about this and that for a while and I knew I just had to wait until he was ready to tell me what he was really here for. Once he had finished polishing the last batch of glasses from the glass washer he came and sat beside me. "You know I have been living with Mum and Dad for the last couple of months sis, well I think I am driving them mad. At their age it must be difficult having me back in the house. They are used to their routine and I am messing that up. How would you feel about me crashing here until I can sort something else out?"

"You know me." I replied. "The more the merrier. It would mean that you would have to sleep on the settee in the lounge upstairs as all the bedrooms are taken but if you are happy with that so am I."

"That's great, thanks sis. Of course I will give you rent. Every little helps doesn't it."

I smiled at him and nodded. If only he knew, at this stage any money coming in was a bonus.

Facing up to reality

We are almost at the end of June and I am sitting in the pub. I am meant to be doing the cleaning. I have not got any music on. The last thing I feel like doing is dancing. The weather in May was lovely but June has been pretty rubbish, just another reason for people not to come and sit in our lovely pub garden.

I spent yesterday evening going through all the bills. Unbelievably the loan I took out has almost gone. I have always had credit cards, the first one I took out when I was in full time work. I was probably about 20 years old at the time. Over the years I have always paid it off pretty quickly if I used it and as a result I presume they saw me as a good risk. The crazy thing is that my credit limit on that card is now £12,000. It astonishes me that at no stage over the years have that bank tried to establish what my situation is. We all have changes to our lives. If I tried to get a credit card now with that sort of limit they would laugh in my face. Whilst I was married I took out a couple more cards, usually to transfer a balance to the new card which was interest free for a certain amount of time. These cards have also gradually increased how much I have to spend. So as a result I have several cards at my disposal. I had been avoiding using them as I know what a trap they can be and I know that if I was advising someone else I would probably say avoid them like the plague but what can I do?

I have already reached the stage where I am not paying my full payments on everything each month. I read somewhere that if you at least paid something they would not be able to come after you. I do not know if that is true but I have little choice. As I am thinking this all through for what seems like the millionth time I find myself wondering if you can be sent to prison for being in huge debt. The idea seems almost pleasant. I would not need to worry anymore. They would look after me. I would get fed and I would not have to think about anything. At this precise moment that sounds like bliss. This is ridiculous I know but I feel so out of my depth.

I know I have to get on with the cleaning but this morning it seems like such hard work, my whole body feels heavy. I really do not know how much more of this I can take. I think Paul and I need to sit down and have a serious discussion about our future but I am really having trouble gathering the courage to speak to him about it all.

It is the middle of July. Several weeks have passed since I sat considering how life might be better in prison. When

I think that I had even been considering such an awful idea it makes me realise what a dreadful mess I am in. I still have not spoken to Paul but the time has come, I simply cannot put it off any longer.

We are sitting in bed and I take his hands in mine and my eyes fill with tears.

"I think we have to go." I whisper, fighting with every fibre of my being not to break down in to uncontrollable sobs."

"Go where?" He asks and my heart clenches. He is sometimes so innocent and his faith in me is unshakeable, he seems to honestly believe that I can move mountains.

"We need to hand our notice in and leave the pub." Saying the words out loud was too much for me and the threatening tears broke free. I put my head down and my entire body started to shake with the emotion of the words I had just spoken.

Paul did not speak, his arms went round me and he held me while I cried. People talk of a broken heart and I think at that moment I knew what that felt like. My chest actually hurt and my head was spinning. There are so many facets to my attachment to this place. First and foremost it was a safe haven for all those that I loved. But it was also my 'baby'. Never in my life had I had something that I was singularly responsible for and the pride I had taken in it was overwhelming. Add to that the building itself and the spirits that dwelt here. I truly love the place. I love every nook and cranny and now I had to say goodbye and the pain of that decision is unbearable. Yet again I have to drag my family to a new home, I know they will understand but it does not lessen the pain I am feeling.

Eventually Paul speaks. "Are you sure? Is there nothing more we can do?" Do you want me to see if I can get another loan?" I shake my head as I put my hand to his face. "It is over, we have done our best but there is really no other option now. I have looked at it from every possible angle and we are finished here. We simply cannot keep pumping more and more money into a sinking ship. There is just so much against us." Paul's chin dropped to his chest and I pulled him to me. This was a rare moment. He always seemed to be comforting me but now I could sense that he felt as broken as I did. He laid his head on my chest and I stroked his face.

It seemed like years ago that we had sat in Glastonbury excitedly talking about one day owning 'The Place'. It had happened far faster than either of us had ever imagined and just as quickly it had all tumbled to the ground.

We laid down and snuggled up, limbs wrapped round each other so tightly, it was as if we were trying to combine our energies to make all the pain go away. My face was buried into Paul's neck and I felt his jaw moving on my head. I could tell he was struggling to speak but having trouble putting into words what he was trying to say.

Eventually he began to speak. "We couldn't have done anymore Sweetheart. You have put your heart and soul into this place. You have worked so hard and everyone else has pitched in, friends and family have been coming in to eat and bring us custom. Everyone has done their utmost to help this business succeed but it simply was not meant to be, we could not have dragged the customers through the door and we could not have envisaged how expensive it would be, to simply be here. You say you have looked at it from every angle and I totally believe that. I know you would not leave this place without fighting with everything that you have: We have to look forward Sweet, I know that probably seems impossible now but it is the only way we can go, we have to go forward and not look back especially not look back with regret. You need to hold your head up high and look to the future."

Fresh tears started to pour down my face. He has such a way with words when the need arises. If I believe in anything; I absolutely believe I was meant to meet this man. The intensity of my love for him frightens me at times but I know that with him by my side we will be fine, wherever life takes us.

Beginning of the end

These past few weeks have been some of the hardest of my life. I did not think it was possible to cry so many tears but every time I have to break the news to someone that we are leaving it starts me off.

The boys were first and then the staff, family and friends and of course the loyal, regular customers.

I read through the contract with the Brewery to see what I had to do and as I had thought I had to give three months' notice in writing. I called the Area Manager and he was very understanding, saying that in all honesty he was not surprised. He told me that he appreciated how hard things must now be and that if I wanted to hold back payment for the drink and rent for the next three months it would simply be taken out of the money from the sale of the business. It was the Brewery's job to find another tenant to buy the business from me and therefore over the next few weeks I was likely to have people wanting to come and have a look round if they were thinking of taking on the tenancy.

I sent in my letter and I had it confirmed that we would be leaving in mid-October. We would have been here eighteen months. I never in my wildest dreams could have imagined that we would be here for such a short amount of time. My blood runs cold every time I think about the money we have lost.

Mixed in with my intense sadness was a sense of relief. At least I did not have to spend hour after hour trying to work out how to make the business work. It was done now, all I had to do was wind it all up and find us a new home.

Having rented a house before we came to the pub I knew all the ins and outs of that process but I was rather concerned about my present financial situation. I know that they do credit checks on all potential tenants and your earnings and I was not sure they would want me. I spent hours going over and over this in my head whilst looking at what was available on the rental market. Properties are snapped up so fast I could not start looking for the next few weeks but I needed to know where I stood so I called an Estate Agent in Witham to ask what to do.

As it turned out it was slightly easier than I had imagined. Paul of course was fine, he had very little debt apart from the loan he had taken out for me. They told me I would not be eligible to rent unless I could find a guarantor who would say that they would cover the rent if I did not pay. I went cap in hand to my Brother in Law who readily agreed to do this for me. Thank goodness! That was another hurdle crossed.

One evening I asked all the children and their partners and Robert to join Paul and I for dinner. I wanted to discuss our plans for the future. I had been having a look at houses for rent and I was keen to hear what everyone's thoughts were on where we would go next. They were all very much in agreement that they wanted to stay local which was of no surprise whatsoever.

Robert was still occupying our lounge upstairs and I asked him what he thought he was going to do, he did not appear to have made any attempt to find somewhere to live over the recent weeks. "If we can find a house big enough would you want to rent with us?" I asked him. If I am honest this was not an entirely unselfish question. I knew that the more of us in the house paying towards the rent etc. the easier it would be. "I will have a think about it." He replied and with that we finished dinner and went our separate ways.

A couple of days later Rob came and found me in the bar. "I have been thinking about it Sis and if the offer is still open and we can find a suitable house I would like to come with you, I am sure my part of the rent will be a help."

"Ok that is great and yes you are right it will certainly help".

Matthew asked me how much I thought his part of the rent would be. I had made it very clear to all three children that they would have to pay a full portion towards the rent and bills in the new house because of our dire financial situation. Up until now I confess I had not been taking much housekeeping off of them as it did not seem right, they were my children and I had always supported them but they were all adults now and working. This is a subject which I am sure gets discussed up and down the land with some parents refusing to ever ask their children for housekeeping but 'needs must' as they say.

Matthew's girlfriend Jodie and Chris's girlfriend Sara were pretty much living with us at this stage and Mike's partner Nick stayed most weekends therefore we were going to have to find a pretty big house.

One morning whilst cleaning the pipes with Matthew he told me that Jodie's Mum had said she would charge much less than me for them to stay at her house. I was shocked. I had not considered this. I honestly had not thought about any of the boys leaving home yet and the feeling that he was having to do this because I was going to be charging more than Jodie's Mum made me feel so sad. To me it felt like just another bad thing to come out of this situation. I honestly did not know whether he would have left yet if he did not feel he had to. Of course this is just my take on it as a Mum wanting to keep her chicks in the nest as long as possible. He may well be very excited at this new chapter for him and Jodie.

I honestly did not think trade could get much worse but to my shock the pub is getting quieter and quieter. It seems word has spread that we are leaving and customers are treating it as if we have already closed. Our regulars are still coming in which is such a relief but our takings are now at dire levels. I am buying less and less from the brewery and our delivery drivers are so sympathetic when I talk to them. They have told me they are seeing it everywhere. These are such sad times for the pub trade as a whole.

My mood has settled down a bit, I think partly because suddenly I have a million things to juggle once more and I do not have too much time to dwell on the sadness of it all.

The Area Manager popped in for a meeting with me and asked why I had not let Lyn, Amy and Pam go. "I only have two months left." I explained. "I know that if they are working for me when I leave, the new tenant has to take them on under the TUPE law and therefore I will keep them on so that they do not lose their jobs." He shook his head in amazement. "In all the years I have been doing this job I do not think I have ever known a Tenant do that for the sake of the staff. It really is very kind of you, if not a little crazy because I know that you surely cannot afford their wages."

I shrugged as I stared at him. "I just cannot do it to them, they all need their jobs. I created this mess. It is not their fault so I will protect them as much as I can."

He told me that there was a couple interested in seeing the pub and that they would be in on the following Wednesday, he asked if I minded showing them round or if he should come and do it. I told him I was more than happy to, I still had tremendous pride in what we had done with the place and despite it not working for us I was willing to show it off. He explained that if the Brewery did not find new tenants by the time it was our leaving date that the Brewery would buy us out.

I tried not to think that far ahead, pain shot through me. I thought I was coping with the idea of leaving but occasionally it caught me unawares. The thought of another couple taking my 'baby' was almost too hard to bear.

My days have become a little crazy. We are of course still running the business so everything I have always done still needs doing but now in addition to this I have to find a house to live in and begin the huge task of winding everything up and getting ready to move. The coffee machine is on lease so that has to be taken away just before we leave. It seems that although I am handing it back there will still be a lot of payments to make which was something I had not bargained for. It is of course in the small print but when I took it on I thought we were here for years so it had not been relevant. Hindsight is a wonderful thing.

What is strange, is that the paranormal activity in the pub has suddenly risen dramatically. Amy got pushed whilst she was behind the bar yesterday. Jo had experienced that when we first moved in but our gentleman ghost behind the bar has been relatively quiet since. In addition to this I keep hearing our little lady in the lobby area between the kitchen and the bar. She had also been very quiet but suddenly keeps making herself known again. I am honestly beginning to wonder whether the spirits are agitated because of our imminent departure.

This evening I am on the bar and Paul is here keeping me company. We have had a few regulars in to eat and the bar is reasonably busy. Before I decided to throw in the towel this would have cheered me up and I would be convincing myself that the tide was turning but today I am just pleased that we will have some takings in the till. It is nearly nine o clock and Lyn has finished cleaning down the kitchen and come to join us in the bar for a drink. Dave and Luke two of our regulars are also here with us.

We have a bell in the bar which is rung from the kitchen when food is ready to be collected for the restaurant. We have it set to the two note sound, not unlike a doorbell. Suddenly the bell starts to sound but instead of the usual tune it starts to play '*When the saints go marching in*'. It was only a few notes but there was no mistaking what it was playing. We all look at each other in shock. "Is there someone in the kitchen?" I ask Lyn.

"Not unless one of the boys has come home and come in the back door." She replies. I jump up and go through the lobby to the kitchen. I look all around and there is no one there. I go over to the bell and press it. The usual two notes sound. I press it again with the same result. Going back into the bar I saw that everyone looked as baffled as me. "Do you think it is faulty?" I asked Paul.

"Even if it is," he replied, "I am almost certain that tune is not on it." I laughed nervously. "Well it must be on there, how else could it have played it?" Going over to the bell Paul pressed a button and it began playing various tunes.

"You press this when you are choosing which sound you want it to play." Paul explained as he worked his way through the tunes. Eventually after about half a dozen it stopped. "That is it," said Paul as he stared at us, "there are no other tunes on it."

"But there must be." I said to him feeling more and more perplexed. He raised his eyebrows at me and to prove his point he ran through the tunes again. We all looked at each other. "Ok, when it rang by itself what did everyone hear?" I asked them.

"It sounded to me like '*When the saints go marching in*" said Lyn. Paul, Luke and Dave nodded in agreement and Paul said "that was what I thought too."

"So we all heard the same tune and yet it does not seem to be on the list of tunes available." I said looking round at their puzzled faces.

"Someone is trying to tell us something or at least get our attention" remarked Paul thoughtfully.

"Do you think it was Paranormal?" Enquired Dave, who after 15 months drinking with us in the pub was used to our beliefs.

"Most definitely," replied Paul, "my attitude is, if it cannot be proven otherwise it must be paranormal, I am the same as Jude, I will look at every other explanation first and if there is none then there can be no other conclusion. If the machine was breaking down it would have just played random notes, it certainly would have not played such a recognisable tune."

As I am sure you can imagine this rather unusual event had us chatting animatedly for the rest of the evening. If nothing else it certainly took my mind off of my troubles for a while.

The following day Pam was setting up the bar whilst I was watering the plants in the pub. "Judith, do you know what has happened to one of the drip tray tops? We are one short." Puzzled I walked over and went behind the bar. Pam pointed to the relevant drip tray. The tray was in place but the criss-cross part which sits in the top of the tray was not there. I thought back to the previous evening.

When the bar is cleaned down we put the drip trays in the dish washer in the kitchen to wash them. Paul and I had cleaned down the bar the previous evening and I had put the drip trays through the dish washer and I know that they were all there when I put them back. Nevertheless I went out to the kitchen and checked the machine. I then searched the kitchen and finally went back to the bar and searched there. As I am sure I have said before I am a bit of a stickler for everything having its own place so the bar and all its shelves are always kept organised and there really was nowhere it could be. I searched in every possible place, probably going over areas that Pam had already looked.

When we moved in to the pub there had been no spare drip trays or tops and therefore I did not have another one to replace it. It was not the end of the world and I was certainly not going to purchase a replacement at this stage of the game. The new tenant could sort it.

As the days passed, it sat niggling at the back of my mind. I simply could not understand where it could have gone and it had not turned up. I had wondered if I had put it somewhere obscure whilst my thoughts were elsewhere but that seemed not to be the case as it would have been found by now.

About a week later Paul and I were having breakfast in the pub. It was a lovely bright September morning and we were discussing going to look at a house in Witham later that day. It was lovely and peaceful and I was enjoying Paul's company and having a little time to ourselves. Suddenly from behind the bar there was a slight bang as if something had fallen to the floor. We both jumped. Paul frowned. "What was that?" I stood up.

"I have no idea, I'll go and have a look."

As I entered the back of the bar there in the middle of the floor was the top of a drip tray. Quickly my eyes scanned along the trays. All the tops were in place except for the missing one. I swung round and stared at Paul. Seeing my apparent concern he got up and walked over to join me.

"Is that the missing one?" He asked as he came in behind the bar.

"Well it must be," I replied, "because all the others are in place. But where on earth did it come from?" I indicated to Paul exactly where I had found it laying. We both looked up and around. There was absolutely no where it could have fallen from. Paul even tried putting it on the glass shelves above the bar and sliding it off to see how it would fall but even though he did it time and time again it was obvious that there was no way it could have fallen from the shelves. In addition to this there was the fact that both Pam and I had searched all of those shelves when it went missing.

Returning to our breakfast Paul was excitedly telling me that he had heard of items going missing and reappearing but he had never seen such a good example of it. So it would seem that for whatever reason our resident spirits had taken it and decided that this morning was the time to return it to us. My feeling that they are upset with us for leaving just keeps getting stronger.

We are going to look at the house in Witham. Chris and Mike are coming with us but Robert decided not to come as he said he trusted that we would find something which was right for us all. We had found one a couple of weeks ago that we all thought would be perfect but at the last minute the owner of the property decided not to rent which had caused panic on my part. We still have about seven weeks until we leave the pub but time is getting short and the amount of places big enough to house us all that are up for rent are few and far between. The owners of the house were very welcoming. I apologised for such a big group of us but they told us they completely understood as this was to be our home it was only right that we all had a look.

It is a town house on a lovely new estate on the edge of town. Just a short walk away is a big duck pond and the house looks out over the fields to the front. What is particularly good about it is that on the ground floor there is a massive bedroom with a large en-suite with a shower and next to that a walk in wardrobe. The room itself could easily work as a bedroom / sitting room for Robert. The next floor up has a kitchen diner which again is massive. It has a waist height dividing wall between the kitchen and the dining area which splits up the two areas nicely. Across the landing from there is a very large lounge. On the third floor is a bedroom almost exactly the same as the ground floor room again with the en-suite and two more good sized bedrooms and a family bathroom. It is perfect and I have everything crossed that we will be able to secure it. The boys are both happy because we are still very close to all of their friends and their places of work. It is also perfect for Robert, I know he would be thrilled with it.

As we drive back towards the pub I realise I have such mixed feelings. Excitement that we may have found our next home but such deep sadness at leaving the pub and total fear at where my life is going to take me next. I feel such a failure, the thought of a new job seems almost too frightening to contemplate.

Breaking Down

It has been an unusually hot day for September. Paul has been my right hand man in the kitchen today and Amy has been on the bar. Just the three of us. Paul and I have been serving in the restaurant as well as cooking as Lyn does not work on a Sunday. We have had so many lovely comments from those that come regularly for their Sunday roasts but it is becoming so hard to even smile and say thank you when I know it is all about to end.

I am so tired. Sadness is definitely affecting my ability to carry on regardless. My whole body aches. Sundays have always been hard work. Getting up at the crack of dawn to peel all the potatoes and veg for the roasts before doing the cleaning in the pub and then doing all the cooking means that by the time everyone has been fed and Paul and I are ready to for dinner, it is almost too much like hard work to eat it.

Today as the weather is so lovely we go out to eat. Sitting together at the back of the garden well away from the last few customers we are both lost in our own thoughts. I have always been a chatter box but I just have nothing to say and the silence is deafening. Paul finishes first and sits looking at me.

"You are very quiet today" he says.

"What do you expect Paul?" I ask. The frustration that I cannot control the tears that threaten, adds to my dreadful mood but I immediately regret snapping at him.

"I am sorry, I know that was uncalled for and I also know that you are as tired as I am. I am just so sad, but you know that and I should not keep referring to it but it seems to overwhelm me the minute I have a moment to think."

"I know," he says as he reaches out to put his hand on my arm. "We are nearly there Sweetheart, only a few more weeks and we will be out of here and starting our new life."

I know it is awful of me but I feel furious that he sounds so relieved. It must have been a pretty strange 18 months for him, holding down a full time job and being here going through all this with me but at the moment I am so full of my own grief at what we are losing I find it hard to be sympathetic to his feelings.

Without saying another word I pick up the plates and march off towards the back door of the kitchen. Paul sits for a while longer nursing his drink. I can see him from the window of the kitchen and he looks so miserable staring at the table but in the state of mind that I am in, I cannot forgive him. 'Starting our new life!' I think, 'how dare he be thinking of it like that?' The trouble is that I do not think of it as a new life. My mind seems to be blanking out thoughts of the future completely. All I can do is think about everything I need to do to arrange the move, wind up the business, keep the pub running until the final day and prepare for the new house. Anything beyond that is a complete blank. Thoughts are raging in my head, a battle between my love for him and acknowledgement that I am being unfair, against anger that he does not seem to be as devastated as I am and can so coldheartedly refer to 'our new life'. I can feel pressure mounting behind my eyes, it feels like my head is going to burst.

We have had a few arguments recently, all over silly little things but I know that Paul hates to upset me and his way of dealing with it is to get angry at himself, which he then turns back at me. It sounds confusing and believe me it has taken me many months to work out the process he goes through but even though I understand it, it does not get any easier when he reaches boiling point. He has the ability to really hurt me with his words which leave me feeling battered. I know this is only because of the mental state I find myself in at the moment but that does not make the actual events any easier.

I carry on cleaning down the kitchen banging the pots and pans like a woman possessed. Eventually he comes into the kitchen and begins working alongside me.

He does not speak. Another trait of his that infuriates me when I am angry. I just wish occasionally that he would try to diffuse the situation by talking to me but it is not his way and so we continue to clean in silence. I know how I am behaving and I should feel ashamed of myself but I am beyond recognising that I am being unreasonable. Every time he puts something somewhere that I would not have put it I sigh dramatically and move it to what I consider its' correct position. After a good hour of this behaviour Paul breaks his silence.

"Do you want me to help you?" he asks, his face a mask of fury.

"I could just piss off and leave you to it, I have done nothing but support you since day one. I think it is time you started showing a little gratitude instead of treating me like a five year old. I am sure many men would just be sitting in the bar having a nice quiet pint instead of slaving away in a boiling hot kitchen with a woman who treats him with nothing but contempt!"

"How dare you." I spat back at him. "Show you gratitude? Do you want me to go down on bended knee and thank you every time you give me a hand? I thought we were in this together!" His eyes darkened as he stared at me and a tiny part of me knew I had gone too far but I was unable to stop the anger I was feeling.

He turned and started to head out the back of the kitchen. I ran towards him and grabbed his arm. He shook me off and I knew that it would not be sensible to try and physically stop him from leaving. He is a big man, much bigger than me. He had never been in any way violent but a person can only be pushed so far and instinct told me to back off.

I stood perfectly still and watched him leave but almost immediately I wanted him to stay. All my anger left me as dramatically as it had arrived and I ran round to the car park to tell him I was sorry and to bring him back but to my horror as I reached the car park he was driving out onto the road at breakneck speed. I ran toward the road desperate to stop him but he was gone.

Watching his car disappear down the hill, all the energy seemed to leave my body. My mind went blank and for several moments I did not move. Then almost without thought I started to walk. I headed down the hill. My mind had gone curiously still. It was as though I had fallen asleep with my eyes open. I was aware of my surroundings but that was about it. The calm that had come over me helped me to recognise that I was walking, I had crossed the road onto the side which had pavement and I was heading towards the slip road to the London bound A12. I reached the top of the slip road and I had the wherewithal to look before I crossed it and then I continued on the old road towards Boreham.

Out of nowhere I suddenly started to scream, tears came in torrents as I screamed and screamed. I was aware that this was happening but seemed quite unable to stop it. My mind which moments ago had been completely empty suddenly filled with all the pain and sadness that had led me to this point. Thoughts seemed to be coming from hundreds of directions all at once, crashing over each other as they rushed to torture me. I began to stumble and toppled off of the kerb into the road. Luckily this is a quiet country road and no traffic was passing at that precise moment as it could well have been my last. Some sort of inner prompting pushed me back to the pavement and I continued on my way, the screaming had calmed when I fell off of the pavement but the tears had not and I could barely see where I was going.

Just as quickly as the storm had hit, it stopped. The calmness returned and the only thought I had was that I only had sandals on. After damaging my foot very badly years ago I have never attempted to walk any distance without trainers on and yet here I was walking in sandals. Some peculiar little part of my brain was concerned about the fact that I was walking without trainers but it certainly did not have the force to stop me.

The calm was very welcome after the intensity of the pain that I had just felt. I did not know where I was going or indeed why I was walking but I kept going. I knew my expression was completely blank, I felt like I had ceased to be. I was nothing.

"Paul went off and left me!" The voice in my head sounded like that of a child and as I heard it the screaming started again as did the tears. The loss of control meant that in between screams I was babbling like a small child. Again I lost my footing and stepped off of the kerb, I did not fall I just staggered into the road. This time a car was approaching and I still had enough self-preservation instinct to get back onto the pavement before I got hit. I did not even see the occupants of the car as it passed me.

The crying and babbling went on for some time before the calm returned with such welcome relief. It was so much easier to not have to think of anything, just an empty mind. "Just walk, just walk!"

By now I was almost into the village of Boreham. The bouts of crying and babbling had reduced and the quiet in my mind returned. 'Where am I going?' I kept asking myself but I really did not know where or why, so I kept on walking.

Once I entered the centre of the village I automatically started to head towards the house of my closest friend in the village. Roma and I had known each other for many years, she gives the best cuddles and my shattered mind just headed towards her.

Roma opened her back door when I knocked and her shocked expression said it all. I did not speak, she just put her arms around me and pulled me into the house. Kevin her husband jumped up at the sight of me. I cannot begin to imagine how my face looked. Pretty dreadful I would imagine if it was anything like I felt.

Roma sat me down and continued to cuddle me.

"What's happened?" she asked.

"We had a row." I muttered through swollen lips.

"Did you walk over here?" I nodded barely able to move my face.

"Ok, let's just rest, Kev can you get Judith a drink of water please." I closed my eyes and rested my head on Roma's chest. No thoughts were passing through my mind, just sadness and confusion.

After some time Roma told me to have a drink.

"We need to get you home." She said as she helped me to stand.

"I won't be long Kev." With that she guided me out to the car.

Driving back to the pub she did not say a word. I sat with my head slumped forward, chin to my chest. On reaching the pub she helped me out and led me to the kitchen door. Paul was in the kitchen. I had not even registered that his car was back in the car park.

"She walked to my house." Roma explained, "I think she needs some rest."

Paul thanked her profusely for bringing me home.

"Let me know if you need any help with anything" she said as she walked towards the back door.

"We will," replied Paul, "and thank you so much again."

We went upstairs. Paul sat me on the bed and told me to wait there, he was going to run me a bath. Still no thoughts were going through my mind other than over and over again 'a bath would be nice, a bath would be nice.' Once he had prepared it he came and got me and helped me to get undressed and into the bath. He washed me, noting as he did that my feet looked a little worse for wear. I did not even seem to be able to dry myself once he got me out of the bath. He dried me and put my nightie on. "Come on," he whispered, let's get you into bed."

As I lay down I felt him pull the covers off of my feet and he started to rub cream into them. That was all I needed and sleep came immediately.

The following day when I awoke Paul told me he was going to get me breakfast. As I tried to sit up he gently pushed me back down.

"You are staying put today, I am going to get you breakfast then I will make sure the pub is clean. When the girls get in they can look after everything that needs doing. I will keep an eye on you and on what is happening downstairs. All I want you to do is rest Sweetheart. I do not want you to worry about anything except resting today." I was not going to argue. I still felt numb. I could remember the events of the previous day but my mind had calmed, I just felt incredibly sad and lost.

True to his word Paul popped in every now and then with food and drinks. I slept most of the day. I was not sure if I was allowing my mind to switch off or whether I had become incapable of thought but by the end of the day I realised I had not been worrying constantly. When I was awake it was as if I was in a strange type of reality where everything was going on around me but I was not really a part of it, like drifting through a strange dream.

The next morning after yet another night of full sleep I felt a little more normal. Almost thirty six hours of non-stop sleep was clearly what I had needed. Paul was still sound asleep when I awoke so I got up and had a long shower. I think I was trying to wash away the misery of the past couple of days.

My mind felt much clearer and I was ready to carry on with all the work needed to get us where we had to go. 'I will apologise to Paul later,' I thought to myself. 'I need to try and stop using him as a punch bag. He is also sad about how things have worked out and I know I should be being considerate of his feelings instead of constantly dwelling on my own misery. He is so caring the way he looks after me and I know I am lucky to have him.'

As I towelled myself dry I began thinking about the events of the day before yesterday. What had happened was clearly not normal and actually very worrying. I hope I am not heading for a breakdown. I need to keep an eye on myself, the last thing I need is to be falling apart and not having the ability to get the business wound up and moved to the new house. Whilst thinking about what happened, it occurred to me how shocking it was that no one stopped to help me. Granted I probably looked like I was blind drunk. I can remember stumbling off of the kerb into the road on several occasions as I was heading for Boreham but even if I did look drunk surely someone would have felt that the way I was behaving was dangerous to myself. But apparently not. Luckily something deep in my mind kept driving me to get back on to the pavement. Thank God Roma was at home to help me.

The Door Handle

As we move into October trade has all but stopped. The bar looks so sad with very little left to sell. I have been reducing my orders as much as I can. When the inventory is done to sell the business, the stock is taken into account along with the rest of the furniture etc. but I already know that I will get very little back when I sell the business. By the time they have taken out the past few months' rent and non-paid bills for drink there will not be much left. I had a call from the Brewery to say that they will be buying me out as they have not found a tenant. It seems a shame but I am sure they will put in a Manager. Funnily enough during our conversation he asked me if I would be willing to go into a pub as Manager in South Woodham Ferrers. The pub badly needed 'turning round' but in my present state of mind I could not contemplate such a task, I am totally beaten and I know my heart would not be in it. I was flattered though to be asked. Even though we had to give up here the Brewery clearly felt I had done a good job of something or they would not be asking me to take on another of their establishments.

The coffee machine was taken away today which has left a bit of a gaping hole on the bar. I have sold some of the leather furniture that we bought for the lounge and we have packed away the last of the items that remained from our market stall and as each item goes my sadness grows. It almost feels like the light is going out of the place. It is starting to feel cold and lost.

This evening I have closed. It is only 8pm but I have so much to do and for the sake of the sale of one or two pints which by this time is highly unlikely anyway, I would rather get on with packing. As is often the case I am alone in the building, Paul is at work and everyone else is out. I walk into the lobby between the pub and the kitchen and pick up the phone. Roma, as you would imagine, has been concerned since I turned up on her doorstep in a total mess and so I have been calling her regularly to let her know I am ok. I sit myself down on the bottom of the stairs and dial her number. Just as she answers the phone a rattling noise comes from the top of the stairs. I say hi to Roma but I am distracted by the noise, I sit for a moment trying to work out what it is. "Can you hear that?" I say to her as it begins to get louder.

"Yes" she replies, "what is it?"

"I have absolutely no idea but I am going to find out, it is coming from the top of the stairs."

"Are you alone in the pub?" Roma asks, her voice dripping with concern.

"Yep, but it's ok, it is probably the cat. If someone has left the doors to the roof slightly open and another cat has come in, it could be fighting with Ziggy."

I said this because the noise had become so loud that all I could think was that they were fighting and banging against the closed door at the top of the stairs.

As I rounded the bend on the stairs I could see the closed door. The handle was going up and down and in frantic movement. I stopped and stared. The top half of the door was glass panelled and I could see that no one was standing there and as I knew everyone was out this was no surprise.

I stood a couple of stairs away from the top staring at the door.

"What's happening?" called Roma, clearly very agitated.

"It is the door handle" I explained. "It is going up and down really fast as though it is locked and someone is trying to get it to open."

"Is it locked?" she asked.

"No, we never lock it. I thought it was the cat, I assumed they were banging against the door but there is no banging coming from the bottom of the door, it just seems to be the handle."

"Get out of there." Roma cried, clearly very spooked.

"It is ok, I am going to go through the door and see what is on the other side."

"Well just be careful, if you thought a cat could have come in the roof doors, could a person have come through there?"

"Not easily" I replied, "I really do not see how they could have climbed up and anyway I would be able to see them through the top glass of the door."

I put my hand out towards the violently moving handle. As I grabbed it, the movement immediately stopped. I opened the door and went through, there was nothing on the other side of the door. The corridor was completely empty. I closed the door behind me.

"There is nothing there." I explained to Roma.

"Well what was making the door handle do that?" She asked sounding very perplexed.

"I am just going to have a look around, maybe it was the wind."

Even as I was saying this I realised I could feel no wind at all. I went straight to the sliding doors to the roof which were closed. We had installed a cat flap for Ziggy and he was nowhere to be seen which did not surprise me as he liked to go and explore the garden once it was dark. I checked every room, there was no one at home which simply confirmed what I already knew and there were no windows open which could have been causing a draft.

"Well I just don't know." I said to Roma. I had been giving her a running commentary of my progress as I checked everywhere. As I started to speak I suddenly heard the noise again. Roma gasped. "It has started again" she whispered. This amused me even though the situation was a little worrying. The fact that she whispered, as though she were here with me. I headed back towards the door and sure enough the handle was going up and down furiously rattling as it moved. I stared at it more fascinated than scared.

Roma squeaked. "How are you even still standing looking at it? I would be out of there as fast as my legs could carry me."

"I think it is because I am sort of used to this type of thing. I know I have never had an occurrence exactly like this but I tend to take it all in my stride. I do not feel threatened at all, I feel perfectly safe, therefore I am assuming that this is not anyone trying to scare me, they are just letting me know that they are here. My gut instinct is that they are expressing their sadness at us leaving. We have had quite a few odd things happen over the past few weeks. I think the spirits in the pub are just letting us know they are unhappy that we are going. The very fact that it is a door that is being used to make contact and it is a door that we would use to leave is quite symbolic to me."

Suddenly the door handle went still.

"You see," I said to Roma "the minute I said that, it stopped, almost as though I have understood and they do not need to make the point anymore."

"Well, you are made of stronger stuff than me," she laughed nervously, "I really could not have stayed there whilst that was going on. Are you sure you are going to be ok on your own there?"

"Yes," I replied "honestly I am fine, I am going to get on with packing some boxes now."

"Well if you are sure, I am happy to come over and give you a hand if you want."

I thanked her profusely and assured her that I was going to be just fine.

"As soon as the move is over you must come and see our new house." I told her, steering her away from the subject as she was clearly much more worried than I was.

After finishing my phone call with Roma I went back downstairs and turned off all the lights. I had locked up and checked the pub before I called her, now I could get on with some packing. Thoughts of the door handle were still uppermost in my mind. I was being truthful with Roma, I really was not scared but I was certainly fascinated. We had had so many strange things happening recently and my feeling that the spirits were sad to see us go had been intensified by this evenings events.

I went into the family lounge and collected a box and headed back to the bedroom, putting the box on the bed I decided to put the television on just for some background noise while I worked.

I had been working for about an hour and was feeling very satisfied with the progress I was making. My office had been the biggest task but I was getting close to finishing in there, all that was left was the essential paperwork I needed for the day to day running of the pub, the handover and everything I needed in connection with the new house. I had spent almost an entire day arranging all the services for the house, booking vans for the move which we are doing ourselves, arranging post re-direction and so many other jobs. I have heard that moving is one of the most stressful things you can go through in life and we are about to do it for the third time in the space of three years, add to that the stress of losing the business and no wonder I am tipping over the edge!

As I pass the bedroom door I hear the title music for the film Pretty Woman, one of my all-time favourites. 'Come on Jude,' I think to myself, 'it is time for a rest. Give yourself a treat for once and sit down and watch the film.' I quickly wash, clean my teeth and get into my Pyjamas and jump into bed. Paul is on nights, I can ring him to say goodnight after the film. He knows I often do not go to bed before midnight.

I know the film practically off by heart so I have not missed much and I fluff up the pillows behind me to get comfortable and fully immerse myself. Suddenly through the door walks the spirit of a little girl with long blonde hair and beautiful blue eyes, she is wearing a long white nightie. I can see her as clear as day, although she is not solid, it is not like looking at a real person but I can see her. She smiles cautiously at me but does not speak, she walks round the bed and climbs up. I am transfixed. I genuinely cannot believe it is happening. The most shocking part is, as I see her climb up the bed it actually dips as though someone has got on to the bed.

"Hello" I say. "Have you come to watch the film with me?" She smiles again but still does not speak, she simply turns and looks up at the screen. I know I have not met this little girl before, not in life nor has she come to me as a spirit.

All thoughts of the film are momentarily forgotten as I begin to think about the fact that this little girl is about the same age as Phoebe who incidentally I know is also here standing just behind my right shoulder. This is a place that I often feel her and also it is where Brian stands. Funnily enough thinking about it I have just realised that the Centaur, that I am still very aware of, also stands behind my right shoulder whenever I am aware of him which I hasten to add I am not tonight, nor is Brian here. Just as well really the room would be getting a little crowded. Whenever I am aware that the Centaur is here he is always quite a way back from me as though he is watching and protecting from a distance whereas Brian and Phoebe when they are in the room with me they stand almost directly behind me.

I realise, as I sit thinking that there seems to be a bit of a pattern forming, for some reason female child spirits seem to be drawn to me. Looking back; the first one I can recall was a little girl in a restaurant when I was in my early twenties. She had literally just appeared next to me. She was about ten years old and she was filthy but beautiful and she had been wearing a very dirty dress. She did not speak to me either and as soon as I took my eyes off of her to look at my husband she disappeared and I have never seen her since. My husband Gerald could not see her and became very agitated when I kept talking about her standing next to our table in the restaurant. Gerald was non believer but after all the years he spent with me and all the spooky things that happened during that time I think he now believes a lot more than he did then.

Then there was the strange night when I had the message about Madeleine Mccann; although I do not think it was her calling out to me it was still about a young female child. Then I had the fabulous moment when the little girl Sandra chose to sit on my lap and now here we are again, a young female child who appears to have just come to keep me company.

A feeling of pure joy passes through me and it occurs to me that maybe the one thing keeping me sane is the presence of all of these spirits. Phoebe most especially who never seems to be far from my side at the moment. I do wonder why I did not feel any of them as I had my horrible experience when I walked to Roma's but I do believe everything happens for a reason and maybe I needed to go through that to somehow vent some of my built up sorrow at losing the business.

Well whatever is going on it is certainly lovely to have this young girl sitting beside me now. She sits next to me without moving throughout the film and as it reaches the final credits the child gets down from the bed and begins to walk from the room, as she reaches the door she turns to look at me. She gives me a gentle smile and the smallest of nods and walks out.

I sit for a while just staring at the door, I realise that I am feeling calm and rested. Maybe this beautiful spirit had come to share some energy with me and for that I am extremely grateful. I think it is time I rang Paul, I feel sure he is going to be thrilled with the tales of the events of this evening.

Saying Goodbye

With just a couple of days to go we have had a little goodbye party this evening with the staff and a few of the regulars, it was so nice to be with them all but sad as well. We had some lovely presents bought for us, one of which was a photo album with memories of our time in the pub which really pulled at my heart strings. It has only been eighteen months but we have had some fabulous times and everyone has been so kind.

We have the keys to the house; I overlapped our dates to make it easier to move out without a crazy rush so we are closing the day before we officially move out. I have taken down all of our pictures and I have already taken most of the plants over to the new house so the pub is really looking bare.

I received a call from the Area Manager earlier on today to let me know that at the last moment they have found a tenant to buy me out. This news had me feeling very odd. I have said all along that I would not want the pub to be empty as I love the building so much but I cannot help a stab of jealousy that this new tenant is going to be running 'my' pub but also that they are going to be benefitting from all the lovely changes we made upstairs. But I cannot dwell on that. I made my decisions at the time for the sake of all of us, to have a nice home to live in. Unfortunately that money spent does not come back with the sale of the business as it was my choice to do up a building which does not belong to me but as I have said before, in my mind it was to be our home for many years, I could never had envisaged this outcome.

Paul has told me to try not to think about that side of things and he is right. We have to look forward now, it brings too much pain to keep looking back.

To add to all the other sorrow is the sadness at leaving the staff. We have become like a little family, we bonded so fast at the beginning that I feel I have known them forever. We will of course keep in touch but I will miss them dreadfully.

As the evening draws to a close I nip outside for some air and if I am honest to shed a few tears. I keep feeling there cannot be anymore tears left but the slightest thing can set me off and the emotion of today has been too much. I cross the road and lean against the fence opposite the pub. My eyes drink in the sight of the building. I know in my heart I shall love it forever. It was my baby, our adventure, our new life and it has gone.

The first landlord recorded was there in 1641. This road was the old Roman Road between London and

Colchester which is why there are so many pubs along the route. They were the old Coaching Inns. So this beautiful building has seen more people come and go that I can begin to imagine. I am sure we will come back one day although I think it will be a very long time before I can bear to cross the threshold again.

As I stare across the road I feel as though I am wrapping my arms around it, wanting to hold it one last time. In my mind I wish it goodbye. I know that the next two days are going to be so full and busy I will not get this time alone to speak to the place from my heart.

'You were my dream and that dream has ended.'

Recuperating

We have been in the new house a week now and I have not stopped. The last two days in the pub after the goodbye party were as hectic as I expected them to be and walking out of the door for the last time was one of the hardest things I have ever done. As we drove away my mind felt numb. My body ached from the exertion of the past few days but also with the pain of leaving. I did not have any thoughts, I was aware of my eyes staring as Paul drove but I was seeing nothing. I knew he had the radio on but it was as if I could not hear the music. I honestly felt like time had stopped and I was not sure how I would ever recover.

And now, a week later, I almost feel as though I have closed my heart to the pain by throwing myself into getting the new house organised. It really is a lovely house and Robert is thrilled with his room. Being downstairs he has his own space and therefore a feeling of independence from the rest of us.

Seeing Matthew moving away was also hard, it seems so strange him not living in this house with us but he is still nearby and he seems very happy and that is the most important thing.

Paul has told me he has a surprise for me and to wait in the Lounge for him. I have tried to think what is about to happen but I really cannot think what it might be.

As he enters the room he is smiling and holding some paperwork.

"I have something for you. It is your 50th Birthday in a couple of weeks' time and I could not let it pass without doing something special for you. Have a look at this."

He hands me a computer printout. When I look at it my heart skips a beat. It is a booking form for a cottage in Ireland. I glance up at him in amazement.

"You have booked this?" I ask. I could not keep the shock out of my voice. No one had ever organised anything like this for me and I was overwhelmed.

"I have booked us onto the Ferry as well, so we can take our car and drive to the cottage once we are in Ireland. I have even booked a bed and breakfast for the first night because it is a long drive to the cottage once we get off of the ferry so I thought it best to rest first."

I feel dreadful admitting that almost my first thought was that we could not afford this with all the debt we have after losing the pub but as if he was reading my mind he took my face in his hands and began to speak.

"I know exactly what you are thinking but it is fine. We are going in November and the cottage and ferry and even the Bed and Breakfast were unbelievably cheap. I cannot imagine that many people choose to holiday in November in Ireland. So don't fret. I wanted to treat you and to be honest I think you could really use a complete break from everything. I have not forgotten what happened to you not long before we left the pub and I never want to see you in that state again. So let's just go and forget everything and just concentrate on each other for a week. I really think we deserve this."

I smiled up into his eyes. What did I ever do to deserve this wonderful man? He is so thoughtful and I am thrilled. The idea of forgetting all that has happened and just letting go of everything for a blissful seven days sounds like heaven.

"Thank you so much darling. You are so good to me. It seems I am always saying it but I cannot stress enough that you keep me sane and I love you so much. It is such a wonderful surprise and I cannot wait to go. You're right it is high time we spent some time alone, we have had very little of that over the past 18 months." I sighed with pleasure at the thought of the holiday to come. I took Paul's hand.

"Come on, let's make some lists of what we need to take."

We are on the ferry! I am so excited I barely know what to do first, part of me wants to go and stand on deck but I also want to explore the ferry. I feel like a little kid, not sure which direction to rush in. So I ask Paul what he would like to do first and he tells me he would love to go on deck to watch as we leave the harbour.

It is November but the weather is being kind and despite a strong breeze we are able to stand and watch the harbour disappear behind us. Paul stands behind me looking over my head and shielding me from the breeze. In that moment I feel utterly at peace and I know he has done the perfect thing for us.

We had a lovely night in the Bed and Breakfast and have driven the 200 mile journey to our cottage. As we enter Paul stops me and takes me in his arms. "Welcome to Ireland, I know we are going to love it here." I kiss him and turn to explore the cottage. The front door opens straight into the lounge where there is a lovely fire burning in the grate. To the right is a small galley kitchen. At the back of the lounge is a tiny staircase. Paul follows me up and we go into the bathroom which is over the top of the kitchen and the bedroom is above the lounge. I do not think I have ever been in such a small property but it is utterly perfect and I am thrilled that he has found it for us. Paul pops back down and brings up the suitcases and puts them on the bed ready to be unpacked.

"Come here." I say to him as he comes back into the bedroom. "Look at this." I signal for him to join me at the window. The view looks out over the bay and the sun is just beginning to go down. "This will be our view when we wake up in the morning. It could not be more wonderful. Thank you darling." His arm is draped over my shoulder and he kisses the top of my head. "I would do anything for you Sweetheart." I knew he meant it. I thought back to how angry I had been in the pub when he had said that he was looking forward to starting our new life. But I understood better now. He had been right. There was no point looking back. I needed to grasp life and all that it has to offer and move forward and I think Ireland is going to be the perfect place to heal and start anew.

It poured with rain during the night. I got up to go to the toilet and it was lashing against the window pane. Any other holiday and I would be gutted to hear that sound but this holiday is different. This is about being together, enjoying each other's company and resting so the rain does not matter and when morning comes and we look out at the most incredible view I cannot wait to see what the day brings.

We had stopped at a Supermarket on the way to the cottage yesterday as we knew we were going to be miles from anywhere so we are well stocked up for the week. For our first day we have agreed to start with a good old English fried breakfast. Neither of us would usually have this type of breakfast but today is different, we are treating ourselves and what better way to start. As we move around the kitchen together I start to sing at the top of my voice "That's not a heaven I'm a singing this sooooong, oooh weee, chirpy, chirpy, cheep, cheep. Woke up this morning and my Mumma was gooooone oooh weee, chirpy, chirpy, cheep, cheep, chirpy, chirpy, cheep, cheep, chirp."

Paul was staring at me with a quizzical look on his face. "What did you just sing?"

"Chirpy, chirpy, cheep, cheep. You must have heard of that I said incredulously." I could not believe that he did not know that song. He started to laugh.

"Of course I know the song, just not those particular words!" Now it was my turn to look confused.

"Those are the words." I said feeling a little indignant, I had been singing that song as long as I could remember.

"I can assure you darling that they are not the right words," he said, barely able to contain his laughter.

"Come on then clever clogs what are the right words?" I asked knowing full well that I was right.

"It should have been; 'Last night I heard my Mumma singing this song'. You sung something about heaven didn't you?" Puzzlement mixed in with his amusement made his face a picture. I thought for a moment.

"That's not a heaven, I'm a singing this song." I repeated.

"What does that even mean?" He asked laughter causing his eyes to tear up. I thought it over in my mind.

"Do you know I have never even stopped to think about it? That was what I thought I was hearing and that is what I have always sung but I have to admit your version sounds more plausible."

That finished him off. "More plausible," he spluttered giving way to full on belly laughing. Tears started to run down his face. He pulled me to him as he laughed.

"I do love you, you daft old bird, I have a feeling I will never hear that song the same again."

We held each other tight, me feeling slightly foolish, him trying to get control over his laughter. I smiled into his chest. Hearing his laughter was such a joy, it seems a long time since we laughed like this together and I had a feeling that this holiday would bring far more.

Little did I realise just how much laughter the day would bring. After our leisurely breakfast we decided to head out for a walk and some much needed fresh air.

I have a love of map reading and enjoy nothing more than studying an ordinance survey map to find somewhere of interest to walk. I had seen a place called 'Eask Tower' which was not too much of a drive away so we decided that would be an ideal place to start.

The boot of the car was loaded up with wellies, coats, scarves, hats and gloves. We had come well prepared for a November holiday in Ireland. Once we were fully kitted out we began the steep climb following the path which led across the sheep fields towards the tower which we could see perched on the top of the hill.

By the time we reached the top our cheeks were glowing from a mixture of exertion and the wind. Nothing could have prepared us for the view or for the blast of wind that hit us as we went over the summit. As the wind hit me I nearly fell over and Paul grabbed me and held on. We stood for a moment hanging on to each other and staring across the bay. The view was fantastic, despite the weather being cloudy the sea was a beautiful colour; add to that the green of the hills with the mountains in the far distance, it was totally breath-taking.

"Come on," said Paul "we can do this, hold on to me." We began walking into the wind, heading for the tower which was a fascinating sight standing all alone looking out over the bay. We finally reached it and leant against it seeking shelter from the wind. Once we had regained our breath we worked our way around it to stand and once again take in the view. Despite the force of the wind a sense of extreme peace passed through me. Holding Pauls hand and staring out at the sea I felt I could have stood there forever.

Eventually rain clouds began to gather and we felt we had been lucky so far but it was time to head back to the cottage. The wind was now behind us and pushing us along at a fast pace.

"Now be careful Babe." Paul remarked as we began to walk back towards the path. "I think we should walk down separately because it is going to be slippery after all that rain last night and if we are holding on to each other and one of us falls we will both go down."

I grinned at him. "We will be fine, just take it carefully."

Our descent was certainly much faster than our climb and I was virtually jogging along in front of Paul. I turned and looked back at him. "See," I called out "told you we would be fine." As the last word left my mouth my right foot slid out in front of me as I hit a particularly deep area of mud. Before I knew what was happening I landed on my side with mud flying everywhere.

"Babe!" Paul's cry of alarm coincided with me hitting the ground with an almighty splat. The sound it made amused me more than anything and I began to laugh partly with shock at first but then as I attempted to get up and slid further along the floor all my strength left me and I dissolved into uncontrollable laughter. I glanced up to see Paul's amazed face which just added to the hilarity of the situation. He smiled and shook his head. "You really are quite crazy." He muttered as he put his hand out to me to help me up.

"Yea but you love me for it." I managed to squeak out before dissolving into gales of laughter once more.

We were literally yards from the car, Paul managed to assist me to my feet and I looked down at myself, the whole of my right side was covered in mud.

"I am going to take this lot off and put it in the boot, I do not want to get mud all over the car."

"You will freeze." Remarked Paul, concern etched into his face.

"I will be fine, I can put your coat round me and we have the heater in the car, come on let's go."

That evening as we sat in front of the log fire blazing in the grate I thought back over our first day. It could not have been more perfect. As soon as we had got back from our walk we stuck all my muddy clothes in the washing machine and then I went and had a lovely hot bath. We played Monopoly whilst our roast dinner cooked and continued on with the game after we had eaten.

"Do you know how much I love you?" I asked Paul. He gave me one of his cute little lop-sided grins.

"I have a fair idea." He replied.

"Honestly though, today could not have been better and I can feel all of the tension of the past few months leaving me. Thank you so much for thinking of this holiday. The cottage and the area are ideal for getting away from everything and giving us time to heal."

Paul nodded. "That is exactly what I wanted Sweetheart, there will be lots to think about when we go home but for now, this week I want you to think of nothing else but being here together."

On waking the next morning and gazing out over the bay I realised I had had the best night's sleep I had had in a very long time and apart from feeling a little achy from my fall I could not have felt better.

It is midweek already and we are having such a fabulous time. Today we have come for a walk at an ancient burial ground where there is a mound which marks where the burials took place. As usual, due to the time of year, there is no one around and we are walking in silence appreciating the history and the intense spirituality of the place.

As we walk I become aware of a voice. I stop and close my eyes; I know that Paul will just wait in silence as he is very in tune with me and will recognise that something is happening. It is a male voice which is incredibly deep. The word he speaks is unknown to me and I try to concentrate on what he is saying so that I will not forget it. "Narvenbragh." The word vibrates through my mind. His voice sounds unworldly, it seems to echo in my head and I feel as though it is being spoken far away from me and yet I can hear it so clearly. It is the only word he speaks and he says it several times and then stops. I wait, not moving, to see if he will say anything else but there is nothing and I can sense that he has gone.

I open my eyes and look at Paul. "What happened?" He asked, always very keen to hear about my latest experience.

"Not much really." I replied and explained exactly what I heard and described the voice as best I could. "I have never heard the word before, have you?"

"No Sweetheart, I have no idea what it means but I shall look forward to looking it up when we get back home." We did not have access to a computer in the cottage and therefore it would have to wait until we were back home in England, so we wrote the word down spelling it out as it had sounded.

The week has rushed by and it is our last day. We have had the most wonderful time, barely seeing a soul the whole week. We have walked every day, seeing the most wonderful scenery. The weather has been surprisingly kind to us, although it has been very cold the rain has mostly come at night and we have had plenty of opportunity to be outside which is where we love to be. Add to that the cosy evenings in front of the fire and we could not have asked for more.

Our journey home was very eventful. A terrible storm raged the night we left. We drove through the night only to find that our Ferry had been cancelled due to the storm. It took us nearly two days to get home but even this could not stop us enjoying every moment of each other's company. We laughed, we sung, we napped and we chatted but as we entered Essex I felt my mind turning to what lay ahead. Shutting my thoughts to everything except just enjoying Ireland had been so therapeutic but now it was time to start looking to the future and finding myself a job.

Good for Nothing

We have been home from Ireland for a few weeks now. I have beenn looking for a job but genuinely do not know what to do. I feel as though I have no particular skills. I jokingly said to Paul that I have reached the ripe old age of 50 and I still do not know what I want to do when I grow up. Although much of my working life has been in offices I feel as though that is not something I want to go back to. Partly because technology has advanced so fast that I feel a little nervy about getting a job in an office where my skills have probably been left well behind. Michael is a wizard with computers and is happy to teach me anything I need to know but my heart is just not in it. I think the work in the pub was so varied and interesting that the thought of sitting at a desk all day does not excite me at all. I know that beggars can't be choosers but I want to be doing something that at least lights a bit of a fire in my belly.

What does not help is my state of mind, this feeling that I am 'good for nothing' clearly stems from everything that has gone on over the past few years and I am finding it more and more difficult mixing with people. I still feel so sad about the loss of the pub but added to that I feel so ashamed. I feel I should have done better and therefore I realise I am hiding away rather than socialising. I would not be able to afford to go out eating or drinking but I could meet friends for coffee in their houses or here at home but I just do not want to. I feel I have nothing to say that anyone would want to hear and I cannot face any questions they may have about what happened with the pub or indeed what I am going to do now.

So because of this bad mental attitude I am spending hours on my own just thinking everything through over and over again. I also spend a lot of time looking at our finances and feeling physically sick as to how we are ever going to be able to pay off all of these debts. I have let the family know that unfortunately we will not be participating in the exchange of presents this Christmas, we simply cannot afford it.

Family members have talked to me about the idea of going Bankrupt but I have always felt that if you cause yourself to get into debt it should be your responsibility to find a way out again. I have spoken to the banks to ask for help with a 'loan holiday'. My idea was that if I could stop paying the banks for a while I could concentrate on paying off the small debts first, i.e. to my pest control man, my Accountants etc. and then I could concentrate fully on paying off the banks. Unfortunately they would not hear of it and therefore I have to continue to try to juggle all the balls at once.

I have seen a job advertised for a Deputy Manager at a local hotel. It is not a big place, it only has about ten rooms so I would think it would be manageable. I am going to give it a try, after all what have I got to lose and for the first time I have felt that this is something I might enjoy.

I realise my hands are actually shaking as I pick up the phone to make the call. The lady who answers sounds lovely and immediately I feel slightly better. She asks me several questions and the interest really picks up in her voice when I explain that I had been the tenant of a pub but had had to give it up. To be honest I am surprised by this. I would have expected quite the opposite but I suppose any experience is better than none.

"Would you be able to attend an interview next Tuesday?" she asks. My heart skips a beat.

"Yes of course." I reply even though fear has made my legs feel a little wobbly.

"That's great." She says. "We really want to get this sorted as soon as possible as the successful candidate will be starting at the beginning of January." She continued on to give me all the details I needed for the day of the interview, informing me that I would be meeting two members of management from the brewery at the hotel. I wonder how Paul will react to this news when I tell him.

As I should have expected Paul was thrilled for me. He was probably also thrilled that I had finally made a move towards getting some form of employment. I had signed on with the Jobcentre when I lost the pub. That had been an experience I would not wish to repeat. I had to have two interviews with them to establish that I was eligible to claim, the second interview was also very much about what they suggested I did to find work. After an hour of talking to an extremely bored looking man he gave a deep sigh and proceeded to tell me that in his opinion I was 'unemployable'. He had come to this conclusion because of the fact that I had been self-employed for such a long time and had owned my own company in the past.

"Anyone looking at you for a job in their company would feel threatened by you. Your leadership qualities are too strong. I honestly think you will find it very difficult to find work as you are basically overqualified."

And that was that. If I thought I had confidence issues about finding myself work before I went to that meeting it was nothing to how I felt now, so it was going to take every bit of my courage to attend this upcoming interview.

As it turned out I coped far better than I would have expected. I have always been aware of my extreme self-confidence and it would seem that in a situation like this I can throw aside all my self-esteem issues and just go for it. I even managed to talk about our time in the pub without crying. As it turned out they were very understanding about that. They told me that at the moment it is being reported that around 52 pubs a week are closing due to lack of trade brought about by the smoking ban and cheap booze being sold by the supermarkets.

Much to my surprise they went off and had a chat together when they had finished interviewing me and then came back and offered me the job.

Paul was very happy to hear that I had got on so well and that they had given me the job there and then.

"The wages they are offering are pretty dreadful." I explained. "I feel like they saw me coming and maybe could also see my desperation to get the job. But to be honest I am willing to take it even with the poor wages, just to get myself back into work and doing something I really enjoy."

"That is exactly right Babe, this will be perfect for you. Just take your time and enjoy it, the wages are not important at the moment. What is important is that you get some of your confidence back working in this trade."

"I am starting on Saturday 2nd January, they said it was a good time as New Year's Eve will be out of the way and I can ease myself in gently as January and February are always quiet months. Apparently the Manager is looking after another hotel as well so he will be in and out but that will be ok. I feel quite excited and the happiest I have been since we were in Ireland."

Paul put his arms round me and held me close.

"You are going to be great, you always come out fighting and I have every faith in your ability to do well. I am so proud of you."

We shall see, I thought, wishing I had as much faith in me as he did. Losing the pub had left me with scars which I know will take a long time to heal.

2010

Today was my first day at the hotel. It was a whirlwind of activity and really a rather strange day, mainly because of the Manager. He was not there when I arrived and I felt like a fish out of water. But as I stood in reception, which I hasten to add was not manned, wondering what to do I recalled my very first day at The Royal Insurance Group when I was just 18.

The head of department was having some sort of crisis when I arrived, she was on the phone crying. I later learnt that she was in the early stages of pregnancy and had just split from the father of the baby. She came off the phone and looked at me as though I had just landed from outer space! Her eyes were looking around the office as though she really did not know what to do with me.

"Right Judith," she said "take yourself off around the building. Find all the different departments and go in and introduce yourself. Tell them who you are and which department you are now going to be working in. That should give me a chance to decide what I want you to do today." And with that she turned away from me and picked up the phone again. To say I was shocked would be the understatement of the year. She honestly wanted me to go on my own and explore the building and

245

introduce myself. The very thought made my cheeks burn with embarrassment. I stood staring at her for a moment but she was already crying again and I realised I was getting nothing more out of her for the time being, so off I went. As it turned out, it was probably one of the most personality building activities I have ever had to do. Everyone I spoke to was horrified that she had sent me off alone to introduce myself and they were extremely welcoming and kind. By the time I returned to our department I felt very much more at home and settled and went on to enjoy 8 very happy years working for the company until I left to have Matthew.

So now here I am again all these years later starting a new job with no one to show me around. Well there is nothing for it, I shall repeat the experience of all those years ago and just explore the place and introduce myself to people as I go.

The morning rushed by and as it turned out I was thrilled to be able to explore the building alone. It is very old, history shows that it was built around the same time as our pub, in fact the similarities are a little spooky. It was an old coaching inn and is steeped in history. It is widely believed to be haunted which Paul will be very excited to hear. Once I get my feet well and truly under the table I will arrange for him to spend some time here with his ghost hunting equipment.

I found my way to the restaurant where two waiters were clearing down Breakfast. I had a long chat with them and learnt a lot about the Weddings that they occasionally hold here. The kitchen staff were preparing for lunch and by the time I got up to the bedrooms the housekeeper was well under way and she was able to show me the rooms, which are all lovely.

Usually when working for an establishment such as this you get your meals whilst you are on shift. However I did not want to assume, so I had brought some sandwiches with me just in case. I was glad that I had because by lunch time I was starving and would not have dared to ask the kitchen for something to eat. So I went and sat in the car and ate my lunch. Paul is off today so I gave him a quick call to let him know how I was doing and then I went back in.

There was still no sign of anyone to show me the ropes. The person running the bar seemed to be acting as receptionist as well and I had a feeling they were a little short staffed. I found my way to the back office and tried to familiarise myself with the paperwork I could see. It felt odd though, as though I was doing something I shouldn't but what choice did I have. I then put my coat on and had a wander round the garden area. It was a bit of a mess and I found myself collecting up abandoned glasses and generally tidying up. It felt good to be doing something practical and as the lady in the bar had no one to help and was keeping an eye on reception as well I felt it was only fair to lend her a hand.

It got to five o clock and a young man arrived to take over the bar for the evening shift. By this time I felt absolutely shattered. Nine to five is not a long time in this trade but for a first day I decided it was enough. I told the chap on the bar that I was leaving and if anyone turned up and asked for me to tell them that I would be in at 9am the next day.

Sunday: I have spent the morning getting to know all the members of staff that are working, several mentioned that they were not surprised that Shane had not turned up to meet me yesterday. It sounds as though he is not the most dependable of people which is a great start I must say. But I will not let his absence deter me. I had considered calling the brewery to enquire after him but I do not want to get off on the wrong foot with him by bringing it to the attention of his bosses that he is not doing what is expected of him. The chef asked me why I had not come to get some lunch yesterday and assured me that it was entirely right that when I am on duty over a meal time that I should get food from the kitchen so for lunch I had a lovely sandwich and now I have stationed myself at the reception desk to read through the rotas and diary to familiarise myself with any functions that we have coming up in the near future.

"Hello Judith." The voice, which came from behind me, had me leaping out of my seat.

"Sorry mate, I didn't mean to startle you." He said as he came up to the desk.

"I am Shane, sorry I did not get here yesterday. I got held up with stuff at my hotel. How did you get on?"

My initial reaction was one of extreme irritation. I had been so busy making myself at home that I had not dwelt too much on the fact that he had not turned up or even had the good manners to make a phone call to apologise and to let me know when he was finally going to be here. However I am sensible enough to know that showing my feelings about this at this stage really would not be a good idea so I smiled politely and held out my hand.

"I am indeed Judith, pleased to meet you. I have been exploring and getting to know the staff and I have spent this morning finding my way round the rotas and diary."

"OK great," he replied as he started to walk away. I was not actually sure if he had even listened to what I said. He turned and looked back over his shoulder.

"Give me half an hour and then come and find me in the office and I will go over some of the systems with you."

Before I even had a chance to respond he was gone. Given my ability to read situations pretty well, I have a very bad feeling about this, his attitude appears to be quite the opposite of mine when it comes to work and I cannot see this going well at all.

By the end of the afternoon my head was spinning. Shane had gone through so many different items at lightning speed. Whenever I learn something new I take copious amounts of notes. I find it is the best way to learn. Also instead of having to keep bothering people with endless questions my notes usually help me work out how to proceed. However he spoke so quickly and moved from item to item so fast I found it impossible to take notes and I felt no clearer by the end of the day than when I had started.

"There we go," he said as he finished explaining yet another baffling system, "I am off now, got to get back to my place. I will be back in on Friday, you should be fine till then. Obviously you know how many hours you are meant to be doing a week. Just add yourself into the rota. If at any time you find you need to cover a late followed by an early just book yourself into a room and stay the night. You will not have time to go home in between a late and an early, especially if the late is a function, you may only get about 4 hours sleep between shifts."

And with that he was gone, leaving as quickly as he had arrived. I was very surprised at what he had said about only getting 4 hours sleep between shifts, that did not sound legal to me but I suppose at this stage I will have to go with it, I did not see that I had any choice really.

The rest of the week flew by. I had not taken any days off which I know was daft of me but I really wanted to settle in and seeing an entire week through gave me a good idea of how everything worked. I have given myself Wednesday and Thursday off next week to have a rest and get things straight at home. Paul has been great on his days off he has caught up with some of the housework and he has been cooking for everyone when I was not there for meals.

I was in the bar polishing some glasses as I got them out of the glass-washer when Shane walked in.

"Alright mate," he called out to me down the length of the bar. "Can you come to the office a minute, I want to introduce you to someone." With that he turned and walked out.

"Good afternoon." I muttered under my breath. "How are you? Have you had a good week?" This man's manners were appalling and every time he spoke to me he made me feel like I was ten years old.

I made my way to the office and was very surprised to find Shane and another man lounging in the office. Neither of them so much as turned to look at me as I walked in. They simply continued their conversation, discussing someone who I assume was a mutual friend from the way they were speaking about him.

Eventually Shane turned and sat up slightly.

"Judith, this is Alan. He is going to be staying here for a few weeks." I felt the look of puzzlement cross my face and I looked enquiringly between them but neither it would appear was going to explain any further. I walked over to Alan and shook his hand.

"Pleased to meet you Alan."

"Likewise," he replied as he turned to Shane. "Right I am gonna get my bags in and get myself settled, see ya later."

And with that he walked out.

"Don't worry about him," said Shane "he won't get in your way, he just needs a bed for a couple of weeks. I will see to it with the brewery so anything he wants to eat and drink he will just settle up with me later."

"Fair enough," I replied, confusion and good manners prevented me from asking any more but my mind was going ten to the dozen. So was Alan a guest or was he going to be working? I really did not understand but decided to leave it as I was certain things would soon become apparent.

It is Wednesday. I have worked eleven days straight and am enjoying a lie in this morning. As I woke up my first thoughts were of the Hotel. It has been a very strange few days with Alan being there. He treats the entire hotel as though it is his home he goes into all areas and seems answerable to no one. I have not seen him do any work and after a couple of days I started asking the staff about him. The answers were all pretty much of a muchness. No one really seemed to know who he was or why Shane felt it was perfectly acceptable to have him staying here and as far as anyone could see there was no money exchanging hands for his room, food or drink. I was told this was not the first time he had been staying here and the previous Deputy Manager was not happy about it either, unfortunately he had left before I started so I had not been able to learn anything from him.

I really should be showing a little more authority on this matter but Shane is higher up the ladder than I am and I feel as the new member of Management within the company that I cannot start flexing my muscles against him.

Although it was good to be at home it meant I had time to sit and look at our finances and as always this sent me falling into a pit of despair. I think I had been able to put it to the back of my mind whilst starting the new job but now going through the paperwork had the usual effect of making me feel a little sick. With all of us paying our way with rent for the house etc. we can keep our heads above water for the day to day living expenses but these debts are just awful. I go over and over it in my mind but there is nothing I can do but carry on paying a little bit to everyone and hope I can keep the bailiffs from the door. It will be a relief when my first monthly pay comes in but I suspect that this will be just a drop in the ocean.

Mental Health

I have been at the Hotel for four weeks now and to be honest it has not been much fun with Alan there. I feel he is watching me, almost spying on me for Shane. It really is a horrid feeling and I am constantly aware of his presence. Shane had told me that Alan was there for a couple of weeks but he has been here for three now and is showing no sign of leaving. I still have had very little training from Shane on the systems and although I am putting through the figures for the brewery the best I can I am not sure it is all correct. Being a bit of a perfectionist this is causing me a lot of grief. I have asked Shane a few times to go over it with me but each time he does, he goes too fast for me to fully take it in. I am gleaning a little more information each time so hopefully eventually I will master it but it does nothing to help my state of mind. Being unsettled in the job and worried sick about our money situation means I feel terribly down a lot of the time. I feel for Paul because I think he thought that our trip to Ireland would 'cure' me of my woes. It most certainly helped me to recover from the dreadful tiredness I felt after the move from the pub and to forget for a while the sadness of the loss but it is never really far away. I try to put it in a box and close the lid in my mind or the sadness of it often threatens to overwhelm me.

Whilst I am at work and Alan is not around I get on well with the staff and throw myself into all that needs doing. Today I met with a lady and her Mother to go over final preparations for her Wedding, which is to take place in the hotel in a couple of weeks. She is very organised which makes my job a lot easier, all I have to do is ensure that everything she wants is put in place and executed throughout the day. I am looking forward to it. I love to run events such as this. I have done it in the past and always had a lot of fun doing it.

So by the time I get home I am feeling a little more upbeat. The upcoming Wedding has given me lots to think about and Alan has kept out of my way today so it has been a little more enjoyable.

Paul and I have been discussing spending a night in the hotel. As it is supposedly haunted Paul is really keen to stay overnight. Shane had said that I should stay if I was doing a late followed by an early but as yet the occasion for me to do this has not arisen. When I do Paul is going to come early evening and I will check him into the room I will be using and he plans to set up his ghost hunting equipment for the night. It is good to know there are some perks of the job and I have assured Paul that as soon as an opportunity presents itself I will arrange it.

Today is a day off and I am at home on my own. I am doing the housework, just basic chores which need little thought and therefore my mind has a chance to wander. I realise I am going over all the bad things which seem to weigh me down so badly at times. As I am working my mood is sinking lower and lower. I cannot see a way out. These debts are going to take me the rest of my life to pay off and the thought of never being free of them feels so soul destroying. I know that if I did not have the grief of the loss of the pub adding to this I might be able to feel a little more optimistic. I have always been so strong or so I have thought and yet just lately I feel as though all my strength has deserted me. Tears threaten and I try to shake them off. I sit down and place my head in my hands and as I do I can hear screaming in my mind. I know this is not paranormal, it is me. I cannot move and as I listen to the screaming my thoughts go back to that dreadful day when I staggered my way to Boreham. This feels the same, although luckily I have a little control over my emotions and I am able to keep the screaming from bursting out of me. I try to make it stop, to make myself think of other things but this just causes the screaming to get louder. I need to sleep, just a little nap to make it go away.

It is the day of the Wedding and I have been at the hotel since early morning. Preparations are well under way and the Restaurant looks fabulous especially with all the little touches that the Bride has requested. She delivered it all yesterday and I have spent most of the morning ensuring everything is exactly as she wanted. I am feeling very pleased with everyone's efforts and notice that for the time being the Screaming Woman in my head, as I have come to call her, seems to be quiet at the moment. The sound has been plaguing me. Every time I let my thoughts wander to the debts it starts up. A horrible wailing sound that makes me want to just close my eyes.

I have told Paul about the Screaming Woman and as you can imagine he was very concerned but I managed to convince him that it is just anxiety on my part and that it is nothing to worry about. This is why I love days like today. We are going to be extremely busy and it will leave me no time to think about anything else which is just how I like it.

Shane turned up just before the Wedding party were due to arrive. Alan has gone thankfully but I do suspect he will be back. There is something really odd about the whole situation. It feels seedy and my gut instinct is that there is a lot going on that I do not know about. This is just something else to worry me. I keep trying to decide if I should talk to someone at the Brewery about it but if I am honest I simply cannot face the drama of it all. I get the impression from the staff that whatever this is, it has been going on for ages so who am I to rock the boat.

I was in the Restaurant when Shane arrived. I was casting a final eye over all areas to make sure that everything was in order and he came sauntering in.

"Wow, Judith, this looks fabulous. Well done." I have to admit for a moment I just gaped at him as I realised this was the first time he had ever really said something nice or encouraging to me.

"Th Thank you." I managed to stammer out. "A lot of it is down to the Bride, she has a wonderful eye for detail."

"Fair enough." He replied. "But at least you have got it all as she wanted, well done." And with that he turned and walked out. He seems to have a habit of doing that, it always makes me feel like he is dismissing me. Like a child being sent from a Headmaster's office.

Before I could give Shane's behaviour any more thought I heard the front doors open and the guests started to arrive. Time for the fun to start.

The Wedding was a huge success and I was very pleased that Shane only stayed for about an hour, I feel so uncomfortable when he is here. Being a hotel the guests are allowed to drink for as long as they wish in the bar and by the time the last of them had gone to bed and we finished the final clearing up it was 3.30am. Driving home, it was all I could do to stay awake. Tiredness was not enough to stop the screaming woman the minute I got in the car. It seems as soon as I stop thinking about work she jumps right in. Luckily I am so tired that I know she will not stop me sleeping when I get home.

The morning after the night before and I feel really grotty, I do not handle late nights well at all and my head feels muzzy. Luckily I have put myself on a late shift today so I have a chance to recover slightly. As always if I have nothing else pressing to think about my mind turns to money and this morning is no exception. My thoughts follow the same meandering path that they always do on this subject because there is nowhere to go so it is a never ending spiral of misery. Suddenly I have the most peculiar sensation, as if I am falling backwards down a huge hole, I can feel myself falling and there is nothing to grab onto, just falling and falling. My stomach turns and I feel as though I am going to throw up. I steady myself and realise that I need to get my mind working on something to stop these horrible feelings. I head to my computer to look up some details I had been thinking about for work.

When I first got up this morning my eye was really stinging but I thought it was because I was still tired from yesterday but I have just looked in the mirror and my eye is red and sore looking. I hope I am not getting a stye, they are so painful but I would not be surprised given how run down I feel. I thought I would start to feel better once I started working but if anything I feel worse. I am still avoiding too much contact with friends and family although when we do get together I do my utmost to not let them see how bad I am feeling. No one wants to be constantly listening to my problems, in addition to which it is natural for people to try and offer advice and believe me if I thought there was a way out of this I would take it but there is nothing to be done.

After two days of my eye getting more and more painful and red I have booked myself into the doctors, I think it needs cream but I want to check with her that it is just an infection.

As I walk into her office she looks at me and pulls a face.

"Oh dear, no need to ask why you have come to see me. Is that as painful as it looks?"

"It is very painful now, it seems to be getting gradually worse which is why I have come to see you." I replied sitting down next to her desk.

"I can prescribe you some cream which will work on getting rid of it but it will also ease the itching and the pain almost immediately you will be glad to hear."

"Thank you Doctor, I really appreciate that." I smiled and lowered my eyes, not wishing to engage any further.

"Is there anything else you wish to discuss? You do not seem your normal chirpy self. I know I have not seen you since you lost the pub which I was very sorry to hear about. I did visit a few times for a drink and you had done a wonderful job with it."

My heart did a little leap, her mentioning the pub took me completely by surprise and my eyes filled with tears. I have known this Doctor for years, all through the pregnancies with my three boys. I am not one for coming to the Doctor very often but obviously with young children visits are a regular thing and we know each other well. But what is it about Doctors and Nurses that we feel we need to share our problems with them. While I think of it you can add Hairdressers and the like to that list.

And so the floodgates opened. I began to talk and felt like I was never going to stop. By the time I had finished telling her about how I came to lose the business I was sobbing uncontrollably. She sat and listened, occasionally offering a small comment here and there and when I finally stopped talking and began trying to get myself under control, she stood and went to her desk drawer.

"I think you may be depressed Judith. I am going to ask you to fill in this form, please answer honestly, it will help me to ascertain whether you are depressed or suffering from anxiety."

My heart dropped. I had long been considering the fact that I may be suffering from depression but I did not want to acknowledge it. Mostly because I do not want to take anti-depressants. It may seem daft but I grew up with a Mother who was very opposed to taking medication of any kind. This attitude had passed down to me and therefore the thought of taking anti-depressants did not sit well with me at all.

She put the form in front of me.

"I am just popping out for a moment whilst you complete the form, do excuse me."

I stared at the paper in front of me. There were numbered questions and to the right of the page two columns of boxes. To each question you had to tick a box to indicate yes or no as your answer. I quickly scanned down the questions and with a heavy heart realised that I should answer yes to every single one. That confirmed it, I was depressed. The question which most shocked me was 'have you ever considered harming yourself?' I was ashamed to acknowledge that I had, I would never actually take my own life but I had found myself at times daydreaming about being hit by a car or some such accident which would be serious enough to put me in hospital. It is terrible to think such a thing but I realise that in desperate times we take desperate measures. I would never do it, I could not do such a thing to my family but the horrid thought raises its' head for the same reason that all those months ago I had been considering how it might be easier to be in prison. My unhappy brain was searching for ways to make things better, to take me away from the pain and clearly it was considering all options.

I cannot admit it, I thought to myself. I just do not want anyone to know how bad I feel. So I began working my way down the sheet. I answered yes to some of the less concerning questions. The Doctor has known me for many years, through the birth of all of my children and there is no way that she does not recognise I have a problem. So if I have to admit to some I will. Hopefully this will create an anxiety diagnosis rather than depression. I feel terrible for being dishonest, I will always tell people that I consider myself an extremely honest person and I am but on this occasion I just cannot do it.

Eventually the Doctor returned to the room.

"All done?" she asked as I handed her the paper. She sat down and began to read.

"So it would seem Judith, that you are indeed suffering from some anxiety as I thought and therefore I am going to give you some leaflets which may be of use to you. If you feel your mental state is declining further then I want you to come straight back to see me and we will look at how we can take things from there. I know you have had a terrible time and therefore no wonder you are feeling the way you do. Please do come back and see me any time you feel you need to talk further."

I thanked her and left her office as quickly as I could, I felt that she could see into my very soul and I did not want to hang around and allow her to see what was really going on. As I walked out of her door I experienced once again the feeling of dropping backwards into the Abyss. I stood for a moment in the corridor and waited for the moment to pass. The Screaming Woman started up louder than I had ever heard her before. I closed my eyes and waited for the falling sensation to stop. As I pulled myself together I began to wonder how this was ever going to end.

Angels

With both Paul and I working shifts sometimes we pass like ships in the night. Our saving grace is that I do the rotas at work and therefore I arrange it on occasion to ensure that we have a day off together.

We both love to walk and we also adore going to the beach. Walton-on-the-Naze is our favourite. We go up to the Naze Tower end and walk down the cliff steps, we then follow the beach as far as we can and walk back up through the woods. It is a lovely circular walk, Paul likes nothing more than to beachcomb and I take photos of anything and everything. This beach was one of the very first places we went for a date. I remember we had been walking and the beach was deserted, it was January at the time and we were wrapped up well against the cold. Paul suddenly pulled me into his arms. As we stood cuddling he got out his phone. I felt a moment of indignation. We were having a romantic moment and he was looking at his phone. However this irritation disappeared the moment the music started to play. He had been looking for something for us to dance to. I honestly do not think

I had ever experienced anything quite as romantic as being snuggled up and dancing on a cold winter's day on a beach.

So today we have a rare day off together and we have decided that a trip to Walton would do us the world of good. I know that I have not been the best company since we got back from Ireland which was about five months ago now. When I am not worrying about money I spend time dwelling on the fact that I really do not know how this man has stayed for so long. I absolutely adore him and I marvel at his never ending optimism and belief that somehow eventually we will all turn this all around.

It is March and it has not escaped my attention that it is two years since we took on the pub. How have we been through so much in such a short space of time?

The beach is very quiet which is just how we like it. Paul is over by the cliffs deeply engrossed in studying something he has picked up from amongst the stones.

I am staring out to sea, listening to the waves lapping on the beach. This is a sound that soothes me like no other and I feel almost trance like as I stand there.

I felt him before I saw him; for a moment I thought Paul had walked up to me but as I turned to him I realised it was Brian. He was standing facing me and my immediate thought, as always, was how incredibly tall he is. He was shimmering and a warmth came over me. I waited for him to speak, realising as I did so, that it had been some considerable time since anything of a spiritual nature had occurred to either Paul or myself.

As I stood looking at him he met my eyes with an intensity which was quite overwhelming, still he did not speak but I knew instinctively that something was about to happen. He gave me a very slight smile and nodded and as he did so he began to turn away from me and the sight that met my eyes literally took my breath away. On his back were an enormous pair of beautiful white wings. I could see the wings in extraordinary detail. It was like nothing I had ever seen before and the shock of it hit me like a wave, I felt a jolt in my chest and a heaving sob burst from me. As I began to cry I dropped to my knees in the sand, the shock of what I had seen had taken all my strength from my legs.

"Babe, Babe." I could hear the concern in Paul's voice as he ran towards me.

"Are you ok? What happened? Why are you crying?" Helping me to my feet, the questions came from him thick and fast.

"It's ok, really, I am ok. These are happy tears, well shocked and happy tears. I just saw Brian." Taking both of Paul's hands in mine as he stood facing me I continued to explain.

"He just appeared next to me, for a moment I thought it was you. He didn't speak to me he just stared at me for a while and then slowly turned." My voice hitched and the tears started again.

"He is an Angel Paul; an Angel, he showed me his wings, they were glorious, so, so beautiful. He seemed to be shimmering as he stood in front of me. The shock of it made my legs go and I fell and when you got to me he had gone." Paul's face was registering the shock I had felt.

"You lucky girl." He said, his expression changing to one of excitement and love.

"Not many people can say they have met a real life Angel. But you say he did not speak? Why not I wonder?"

"I have no idea, maybe for whatever reason he decided the time was right to let me know of his status on the other side. I wonder if all Angels are so tall. It has always seemed odd to me, the height of him. Although I have never given it a great deal of thought he must be at least 8 feet tall, much bigger than we are."

"What did his wings look like? Can you describe them?

"More beautiful than you ever could imagine. And so detailed. White feathers as you would imagine but what struck me in particular was the top of the wings there was a darker part which seemed to run right across the top of them."

Paul pulled me to him and we stood, clinging on to each other, both lost in our own thoughts as the waves continued to lap the shore around us.

As we drive home Paul is making me laugh. I think it is his ability to amuse me and his unwavering support that has kept me from completely losing my mind. Even in the darkest times he manages to do or say something which sets off a burst of hilarity between us.

"Have I ever told you the tale of my previous dealings with the Angels?" I asked him.

"I don't think so Sweet, tell me about it." He smiles at me and as usual for a brief moment the world stops. He melts my heart.

"It was years ago, the kids were all still at the school in Boreham. I was on the Schools' P.T.A. and we were in the middle of preparations for the Summer Fete. I was at home in the lounge and I was on the floor with stuff all around me. I think I was making up some sort of goody bags for prizes for one of the stalls.

I had the telly on to keep me company and Richard and Judy were on which shows how long ago it was! They said that their next guest was an Angel expert. My ears pricked up as they always did when anyone talked about anything spiritual. I stopped what I was doing for a while to concentrate on what this woman had to say. One of the things that she explained was the appearance of white feathers. This is supposed to be a message from the Angels.

Either just to let you know they are near or to let you know that if you have had a hard decision to make and you have decided what to do and then you find the white feather it is the Angels letting you know that you have made the right choice. So me being me when she had finished talking I got up and had a wander round the lounge and whilst I was doing so I was thinking to myself that I needed to find my white feather, so that they would let me know they were around. Much to my disappointment I found nothing.

Later on that day I had to go to Witham. This involved going down to Hatfield Peverel and joining the A12. This slip-road is a bit hairy because there is a slight bend on the A12 before the slip-road, so it is difficult to see far beyond the bend to see what is coming, which makes it a bit of a gamble joining the fast moving traffic.

I let a lorry pass and then slipped in behind him. As I did so my entire windscreen became obliterated by white feathers. This was momentarily terrifying as I was blinded, I am not joking the whole windscreen was covered by feathers. Naturally they blew away almost immediately and I could then see that the lorry I had come out behind was carrying Chickens."

At this Paul bursts out laughing. I wait for him to recover and then continue on with my story.

"I can see why this would make you laugh, it had exactly the same effect on me but as I was driving I began to wonder. That lorry had been travelling along the A12 for some time as it was a few miles back to the previous slip-road so why at the precise moment did all those feathers come out and in all the years I have

272

been driving and seeing lorries carrying chickens I have never seen something like that happen. Yes you see the odd feathers blowing out, it is inevitable with loads of cages of chickens on board but this was enough to completely cover the screen, there must have been hundreds of them. The more I thought about it the more I was convinced that the Angels had given me a sign. In fact it felt as though they had yelled at me that they were most definitely around. But the story does not end there.

The next day I went to work. I worked part time for a company which made electrical parts. At lunch time I would cover the switchboard in reception. There was a coffee machine near where I sat and every time I was there a particular delivery driver would come in. He always sat with me and had a coffee and over time we discovered that we had a lot in common. We both loved the paranormal and we both had weird and wonderful dreams which we used to tell each other if we had had one the night before.

On this particular day he came in and I said to him that I had had a very odd experience the day before. I went on to tell him my feather story and as I talked he was slowly losing the colour in his face. By the time I had finished he was looking quite ill. I asked him if he was ok and he then told me a tale which in turn blew my mind.

He had taken a day off of work the previous day. He told me that he had a very personal problem and he needed to make a decision as to what he was going to do about it. He had gone to play a round of golf on his own as that day the final decision *needed to be made. He wanted to play golf on his own as it would help him to relax and think everything through. By the time he reached the final hole he had made his mind up as to what he should do.*

He was on the green ready to take his final putt. He had looked at the hole and lined up the shot. As he went to hit the ball and his eyes went back to the hole there was a large white feather on the green. He said that it literally seemed to have appeared out of nowhere because when he had been lining up the shot seconds before it was not there and he was absolutely certain that he would have seen it fall if it had dropped from the sky because it was so big. He walked over and picked it up and put it out of the way to the side of the green. He then finished his game and headed for home and did not really give the feather a second thought until today.

Apart from anything else it was so odd that we had each had our feather experiences on the same day. But he was absolutely certain that my story had happened not for me but for him. He was thrilled to have been given a sign by the Angels that the decision he had made was the correct one.

Driving home that day I was thinking about the entire story and had a really strong feeling that he was correct. Although I now fully believed in the existence of Angels what was even more intriguing was that I had appeared to be the messenger. As if I had been used by the Angels to get this message across to my friend.

274

Nowadays of course, I know that I can pass messages on and so this idea seems perfectly acceptable but at the time it did rather blow my mind."

"I can imagine it did Sweet," said Paul as I finished my story, "you really have had a lot go on haven't you. I would imagine the Angels and the sprits had been pulling their hair out until I came along and woke you up to your gifts."

"That is the strange thing though Paul. I honestly never imagined that there was any more to it than knowing that odd things happened to me. I think because I had not really had anyone around me who understood it all, I had never questioned it."

The entire journey home is a mixture of laughter and bouts of chatter about the simply amazing occurrence on the beach. By the time I get into bed I am feeling more rested and happy than I have in a long while. I feel as though I just need to hang on to the lovely thoughts of today and not allow anything else in as I drift off to sleep.

No End in Sight

I am doing a late followed by an early tomorrow morning. I have booked a room so that Paul can have his ghost investigation. Shane has gone away for a few days so this is the ideal opportunity. Although he has told me it is ok to book a room I still prefer to do it whilst he is out of the way.

I have been here two and a half months now and I have mixed feelings about Shane because I am frustrated that I appear to be doing his job for him and yet I am doing it on Deputy Manager wages, which I can guarantee are much lower than that of a Manager but at the same time I prefer it when he is not here. Alan seems to just come and go as he pleases and I still cannot get my head around what they might be up to. One thing I am fairly certain of is that none of Alan's bills are being paid. He just uses a room, drinks what he likes and eats what he likes and yet I do not see any tally being taken of what he is consuming, nor does anyone seem to keep a note of how many nights he uses a room. He just picks a room when he arrives and uses it until he is ready to leave and no one seems to bat an eyelid.

I am also getting a little fed up with the Head Chef. He is another one who is a rule unto himself. He is often not around and I tend to wonder if he is moonlighting at another establishment. The kitchen never lets us down because they are a very good team but the inconsistency with the Chef bothers me. Unfortunately Shane is very unapproachable and is here so rarely that I do not really know how to address any problems I may have.

All of this is making me feel as though I am not doing my job properly and as a result I feel really uncomfortable. When I first began the job I was so excited to be coming back into an industry that I love but lately I am starting to feel like I am wading through treacle. In general the staff are lovely but it feels very dis-jointed whereas in previous establishments where I have worked the team has felt almost like a family. In most places there is always a little friendly banter between front of house and kitchen as they work as separate teams but on the whole I have always loved the team spirit, it is one of the perks of the job to work in such a happy environment. But I am not feeling it here, there is something lacking which I cannot quite put my finger on.

During my time at the Hotel I have been into all of the bedrooms as I like to be able to talk knowledgeably about the hotel to any potential guests and I have been looking out for anything paranormal but there was only one room which did not feel quite right, in fact I was very quick to exit that room. I know that Paul would want to stay in that room but I absolutely cannot face the idea of spending a night in there so I have booked us into one of the other supposedly haunted rooms. He is so excited and I hope he gets some results from it. I have warned him he will not see much of me this evening but he is fine with that, he will be in seventh heaven surrounded by all his ghost hunting equipment.

Paul and I agreed that he would have dinner at home before he came to book in as I would not be able to eat with him here at the hotel, even though I am allowed a break I would not be comfortable trying to spend time with Paul whilst I am supposed to be working. It was a lucky decision as I have been really busy today, I managed to grab a sandwich at lunch time but now I need to have a quick bit of dinner before Paul arrives and I start a shift on the bar. The chef is his usual cheery self when I go to the kitchen and ask for some Lasagne. I have to bite my tongue and not get into an argument with him over his bad attitude.

When he finally brings my meal out to me it barely feels warm and I wonder how long he gave it when he heated it up. But I really do not have time to ask him to heat it through so I quickly eat it up and head off to the bar.

It is quiet in reception when Paul arrives which I am glad about because the amount of bags he has brought in would look a little strange to anyone watching. I think he has absolutely every bit of equipment he possess bless him. I take him up to the room and give him the key and tell him I should be up at around Midnight.

The bar is busy all evening and by the time we have cleaned down it is 11.45pm. I had not been far wrong in my prediction. When I get to the room Paul is laying in the middle of the bed surrounded by cameras and recorders and trigger objects. The sight of him makes me laugh.

"Happy are we?" I ask as I sit down beside him and sigh with relief as I take off my shoes.

"I have not really felt anything yet, he says, none of the sensors have gone off but it is early days and the recorders may have picked up E.V.P.'s which I will not hear until I play them all back."

"Well I am going to have a quick wash and get into bed, I am absolutely shattered, it has been so busy down there and I need to be up at 6am for the Breakfast shift."

"That's fine Babe, we knew we would not spend much time together, I am just really pleased to be able to have this chance to investigate the room. Get yourself into bed, I will give your back a rub whilst you fall asleep."

I had just laid down when a dreadful pain ripped through my stomach. It was so sudden that I jerked up into a sitting position.

"Are you ok Sweet?" Paul looked at me in alarm.

"Hells Bells that hurt" I replied, "I just had a horrible pain in my tummy." As I was speaking it happened again only this time I had the horrible feeling I was going to be sick.

"Oh no, I really hope this is not because I ate some Lasagne that had not been heated through."

"When did you do that?" Paul asked as I tried to get myself into a comfortable position.

"This evening, I was in a rush at dinner time and I did not want to bother the chef by telling him it was not very warm, it seems to have passed though, I am sure I will be fine."

"I hope so Babe, you don't want to be sick in here."

I snuggled down and tried to ignore the pains in my stomach. I thought maybe it was not helping that I was so tired. If I got some sleep maybe it would pass.

I did fall asleep but at 4am I awoke and although the pains were not so sharp they had now become a constant ache. I laid staring at the ceiling with Paul snoring gently beside me. By 5.30am I decided I might as well get up and get ready for the day. I went into the en-suite for a shower and by the time I came back into the room Paul was up and dressing.

"I am going to go home and have a shower and breakfast, get out of your way so that you can get on with your day".

"O.K. darling but to be honest I have a horrid feeling I will not be far behind you. I have just been to the toilet and believe me it was not pleasant. It is not going to go down well with the staff if I leave them in the lurch but I should not work on Breakfasts if I have an upset stomach. I think it was the Lasagne but I cannot take the chance that it is not a bug."

"Alright Sweet but are you going to be ok to drive home? You could come in my car and we can leave your car here."

"No, I have just been to the loo so I am sure I will be fine. It is only a 20 minute drive, I just want to get home because I am starting to feel really grotty. I am going to let the staff know that I am not going to be here today. If you get all the bags down and leave your key on the front desk, one of the staff with sort it out. I will see you at home, I am not going to kiss you just in case I am infectious."

Paul was still packing the car when I left. Giving him a quick wave I shot out of the car park. Driving home I began to wish I had taken up Paul on his offer of a lift. I had my teeth tightly clenched as I had a terrible feeling I was going to be sick any minute. The pains in my tummy were really starting to kick in now. Although it had been a constant dull ache it was now becoming regular sharp griping pains and I was feeling weaker by the minute. I knew I was driving too fast but I just had to get home.

Reaching the house I could not get through the front door fast enough. It seemed like I was climbing Mount Everest as I rushed up the stairs to the top floor and into our bedroom.

By the time Paul got home and came up to see how I was I had got myself into bed having been sick and to the toilet again.

"Oh Babe, you look awful, you are as white as a sheet. Do you think I should get a Doctor?"

"No, I will be fine, I just need to sleep. I feel so weak but now that I have been sick hopefully it will begin to pass."

"Well if you are sure I will just leave you to sleep it off but I will come up every now and then to check how you are doing."

"Thank you darling, oh God, watch out!" I jumped out of bed and headed back to the en-suite.

"Get me a bucket please I called as a fresh bout of sickness overcame me." He was back within minutes and handed the bucket through the door, by now I was on the loo and so glad I had asked for the bucket as a fresh wave of sickness overcame me. I have had food poisoning before and I was almost certain that this was what I was suffering with. I heard Paul opening the windows in the bedroom. Poor man, he is so attentive. I am sure many men would have been running for the hills at this stage.

Two days have passed since the sickness started. Paul has been caring for me so well but I am as weak as a Kitten. I have not been able to do anything for myself other than get to the bathroom. I have been having sips of water but even this seems to make me sick again. I say sick, by now I am empty so it is literally whatever I try to take in just comes straight back up. Paul has asked so many times if he should get a Doctor but I keep hoping it will pass. I really do not want to trouble anyone, I will be fine.

Mum came to see me today, she looked so worried.

"We have had food poisoning before Mum, you know what it is like. I just have to wait for it to get out of my system."

"I know, but you look so ill Jude. Are you managing to keep anything down at all?"

"No but it is not long since it started; give it time."

"My biggest concern is that you will very quickly become dehydrated, you must try to keep something down. I will get you some of that stuff you can get from the chemist, it is a powder you mix with water and drink it to replace the salts in your body."

"O.K. Mum, do whatever you think is best, I just need to go to sleep."

"Alright, I will get some and come and see you tomorrow."

"It has been five days now and I cannot believe that I still feel so weak."

Mum smiled, "I know but you are at least looking slightly better and thank goodness you are managing to hold some water down now. I think you probably should have gone to hospital you know, you are such a stubborn Mare."

"Well you have been here every day and I knew that if you really thought I needed it, you would have called an Ambulance."

"True. Has Shane called today?"

"Honest to God Mum, he is driving me mad. I feel like saying to him, 'do you want to come and look at me to see that I am not making it up.' He has called me every day to ask what is happening. I honestly think that he would get into trouble if the Brewery knew how he was hassling me, it cannot be right to be doing this. It is only because I was running the place for him and he is probably having to do some work now!"

"Alright, calm down you will wear yourself out, I don't want you going down-hill again. I will come back tomorrow. Thank goodness Paul was off when all this started, now that he is back at work he has given me a key so that I can come in and get you whatever you need."

"He has been such a darling you know, he has been washing me, like a bed bath each day because I can barely get to the loo without collapsing. I am hoping that in a few days I will have the strength to have a shower."

"Well don't rush it, you will be very weak for a while after not eating or drinking much for so long."

"I am going to look like a cream cracker by the end of this. At the moment it is all I fancy along with drinking water."

"At least it is something, you will soon get there. I am going to go now, is there anything you need before I go?"

"No thank you Mum, I will be fine, I really do appreciate all you are doing for me. See you tomorrow."

Just a short visit from Mum leaves me thoroughly exhausted and as she leaves I fall straight back to sleep.

"Your Mum rang this morning" Paul said as he straightened the bed around me. "She was checking how you are, she said she will pop over and see you again when I am back on shift in a couple of days."

"O.K. I will text her later, I just need to sleep first."

"You have only just woke up Babe, I am getting worried about you. You still seem so weak, it has been 10 days now and you are managing to eat more. Do you think you should try getting up for a while?"

"Not yet Paul, you know how I wobble just having a shower. I really can't. In a day or two maybe. I am so glad Shane has given up on his daily calls. I think I finally managed to convince him that this had been serious and it will be a while before I go back." Sitting down next to me on the bed Paul began to stroke my hair. I closed my eyes, grateful to be able to shut out the World once more and drift off to sleep.

Brian

I wake and glance at the clock, it is 2pm. A fresh drink and a sandwich covered in cling film are on the bedside cabinet. Bless him, Paul is so good to me. The boys and Rob have all been popping in occasionally to check on me throughout the illness and I feel so grateful to have them all around me but even that does not stop the clouds immediately forming in my mind. I am beginning to realise how much easier it is to just lay here and hide from everything. The Screaming Woman starts as soon as I begin to think, since I have been ill she has been a little quieter, probably because she has not been quite so troubled whilst I have been too ill to think. The feeling of falling into the Abyss has also lessened which is a great relief as that is almost unbearable, it is like nothing I have ever experienced before but then mentally I have never been in such a dreadful state before.

Having said all of that, the very fact that I am thinking this shows that I cannot hide here much longer. My mind is getting sharper every day and the thought of getting out of bed and allowing the screaming woman back in is almost too much to bear. Paul has been so patient, he knows how low I have become and I know that he simply does not know what he can do to help. Frankly I don't think anyone can. I got myself here and I just do not know what to do. I cannot bear to think about the debts, the very second they enter my mind my stomach drops and I immediately start thinking about how much I am hating my job. I feel trapped because I need to earn money to pay the debts but Shane is becoming unbearable to work for.

I drop backwards into the Abyss and the Screaming Woman reaches a crescendo. I close my eyes desperate for sleep to stop all the ghastly thoughts rushing through my mind. If only I could stay asleep and never wake up, it would be so much easier. Tears begin to flow and I have not even got the energy or inclination to wipe them away. 'I am done' I think to myself, I cannot go on anymore. I don't want to ever have to get out of this bed again.' My heart lurches as I think these horrible thoughts but I cannot fight them. I just need to sleep, it is the best way to get away from my mind. All those around me that love and care for me would be horrified if they really knew my state of mind. I always manage to put on a brave smiley face when they are around. It is like wearing a mask, covering the pain, grief and shame that the past two years have brought to my door. I find myself wondering what I have done to deserve this level of sadness. Only Paul truly understands and even he would be a little shocked to hear my thoughts of wanting to just go to sleep and never wake up.

I eventually ate the sandwich when my stomach started to moan at how hungry I felt and Paul has now come to bed. The darkness in the room is very welcome as I can hide my eyes from him. He knows me so well and I think he would be shocked to see that I have hit an all-time low today. The only problem with sleeping all day is that when night time comes I am suddenly wide awake. I don't want to be however because if I am awake I can think. The same thoughts as earlier begin their unending journey around my mind and I feel my body weighed down with the pain of it all.

Suddenly I am aware that Brian has come into the room. He is standing by the bed and telling me to not be frightened. It never ceases to amaze me, how tall he is, he is such a huge presence, he seems to glow and shimmer which is wonderful to see. He says he is going to lift me up. Somehow this does not seem strange and I allow him to do so. I am laying on my side and he scoops me up almost as you would a toddler. As he picks me up I realise that I need to put my arm across my chest and into his chest or it will simply flop backwards. As I do this I glance down and I see myself on the bed putting my arm up across my chest...... At that moment I realise I am out of body, shock jolts through me but before I really have time to consider what is happening I realise Brian is standing on a cliff.

I look around and the first thing that strikes me is that there is clearly a storm raging from the look of the sea and yet I cannot feel a thing. It is as if we are in a bubble which is protecting us from the wind.

The sea is frothing and the waves are immense. I have never seen anything like it. The cliff Brian is standing on seems to go for miles and all around us is just grass. The cliff is so high above the sea and it crosses my mind that I am so glad we are in our bubble as I am sure the wind would blow us straight off the cliff and into the raging sea. Brian is still holding me like a baby which is immensely comforting and does not feel at all strange. After a few moments he speaks to me.

"What can you see?" His question surprises me and I take another look at our surroundings. I tell him about the cliff and the sea and that there is a storm raging.

"Look up." He says, and as I do so my heart seems to stop. Above us, flying in all directions are Angels, dozens of them. A tingling sensation runs through my body and I feel all the hairs on my arms stand up.

"What do you think they are doing?" Brian asks.

"Well it certainly looks like they are having fun." I reply. I can feel the look of wonder on my face as I gaze at this incredible sight above me.

"Yes, they are enjoying it. Do you see the large muscle I have at the top of my wings?" I did not need to look, it was something I had noticed when Brian had shown me his wings that day on Walton beach.

"Yes I know the muscle you are referring to."

"It is this muscle that allows us to open our wings to fly. It needs exercise, like all muscles do and so although they are having fun they are also doing exercise for their wings." I nodded in awe as I watched this truly unbelievable spectacle.

"The reason I brought you here Judith is to show you this because I want you to understand that in order to strengthen your wings you have to fly through stormy winds."

The final word had barely left his lips and suddenly I am back in bed. Lying on my side with my arm still tucked into my chest. Gasping, I pull in as much air as I can. It almost feels as though I had been holding my breath. For a moment I simply cannot take in all that had happened. Very quickly I become aware of feeling as though I am glowing. That is the only way I can describe it. My body seems to be pulsating with energy. I feel warm and thoroughly energised but most of all I feel incredibly peaceful. My mind is clear and I barely dare think in case I lose this marvellous feeling. The joy I am feeling makes me want to cry out but I do not want to wake Paul. I close my eyes and think back to the words that Brian spoke.

"In order to strengthen your wings you have to fly through stormy winds."

A New Dawn

s I open my eyes I realise I have slept all night which is unheard of for me, I always have to get up for the toilet. Paul is fast asleep. The events of last night hit me with a jolt and last night's feeling of joy overcomes me once more.

Generally I would never wake Paul without good reason but this is too urgent. I need to start my new life now! Gently I touch his arm, not wanting to make him jump or worry him.

"Paul, wake up, I need to talk to you." Bless him, his eyes shoot open and immediately concern covers his face.

"Are you ok Sweet?"

"I am fine, more than fine, I am wonderful. Last night Brian came and got me, he took me out of body to a cliff and the sea was going mad and there were Angels, dozens of them and Brian spoke to me and made me see that I have to fight, I have to make things right." The words were spilling out of me, barely making sense as Paul stared at me in shock.

"Slow down Babe, tell me slowly what happened. Brian picked you up? Oh my God, were you scared?"

"No, that was the strange thing, I felt so calm. Honestly I cannot tell you how it felt, it was the most amazing thing and when he brought me back I was glowing, pulsating, it is so hard to explain." Paul slowly began to smile.

"Calm down Jude, you are going to blow a gasket if you carry on like that. It is so good to see you like this. Your eyes are sparkling again, I do not think they have sparkled for a very long time now."

"I need you to help me Paul. I will explain it all fully later but I really need to do this now. I want to shower and dress and I am going to type a letter and I want you to take me to the Hotel so that I can hand in my notice. I only have to give a week and I am still so weak I could not go back to work yet so I am going to put in the letter that I will be working out my notice period whilst I am on sick leave. I am never going back there again. And then I am going to find myself an insolvency practitioner to help me with the debts." My breathing is coming in quick gasps as I rush to say all that I am feeling.

"Ok, ok, come here and have a cuddle whilst you calm down. Please don't forget how unwell you have been and how weak you are. As soon as you calm down I will help you get ready and you can do your letter." Paul took me in his arms and I sighed as he held me.

"I cannot hear the Screaming Woman." I whispered as he held me. "I hope she has gone." I could feel Paul's head nod above mine.

"I suspect she has Babe. Brian has chased her away."

Shane is not at the Hotel when we get there, what a surprise! I give my letter to a member of staff and explain. I ask her to call Shane and let him know that I have given in my notice. I hope the next Deputy Manager has more strength to stand up to him and to deal with the peculiar Alan situation which I never got to the bottom of but thankfully this place is no longer my concern. I have bigger fish to fry.

When I get back into the car my legs are shaking with the exertion of having stood for longer than I have in nearly two weeks.

"Let's go home." I smile at Paul as I say this. I cannot believe how much better I feel, not just physically but mentally as well.

"I think that is enough for one day, I will start to look for someone to help me with the debts tomorrow. For now I just want to go home and rest and enjoy the feeling of being able to relax without the Screaming Woman jumping into my head."

"Just take your time Babe, you have jumped the biggest hurdle, leaving that job. I am sure someone will be able to help you get the debts in order. I trust you to be able to sort it, you always do!"

As usual his complete faith in me brings tears to my eyes, but I know he is right, with Brian's push in the right direction I am going to get this sorted. It is time to take control.

A week later, having fully regained my strength, I have just come out of the insolvency practitioner's office. After much discussion and me detailing how the finances stand he has suggested that I go Bankrupt. This was shocking news to me, I thought he would have a way of paying the debts off gradually but he managed to make me understand that it was not my fault that the business failed with all that I had going against me and that many people go Bankrupt for simply overspending on their credit cards. He told me that I could hold my head up high, for in his eyes I had done nothing wrong and in fact he was impressed that I had paid off all of the little businesses and they would not lose out on the Bankruptcy. He warned me that when I went to court the Judge would give me a bit of a telling off. He said this was normal as they need to try and ensure that people will be more careful in future.

I have loads of paperwork to fill in and once I have filed for Bankruptcy and all the paperwork is with the courts they will send me a date to appear before the judge.

In the meantime Paul has told me to forget about looking for another job until this is done. He says that after being so ill he wants me to take things easy and deal with one thing at a time. I can understand his concern as I do not want the Screaming Woman to come back and neither does he. I am still experiencing a mild version of falling into the Abyss. When I find myself thinking about the debt and my impending court date my tummy does an impressive amount of flips but even that is a relief in contrast to the Abyss.

I definitely feel a lot brighter and am constantly amazed that the experience with Brian has had such a huge impact on how I am feeling mentally. I have not given too much thought to the Spirit World lately. I am sure that will come back once I have sorted everything out.

I have been completing all the forms and the final thing I had to do was write a statement for the Judge to read before he looks at all the ins and outs of my finances. It was hard to write and I found myself crying as I went over everything that had happened. One huge relief is that I took the decision at the time of taking on the pub of doing everything in my name. As Paul had kept his job it seemed the right thing to do then and I am so glad I did.

This means that in the future only my name will have the Bankrupt decision tied to it.

The Insolvency Practitioner explained to me how this will effect everything I do with regard to finances for a very long time, in some cases forever; but I am prepared to accept that as I cannot live with the pressure of the debts anymore. I will only be allowed to have a bank account which I can draw cash from so that I have somewhere for a future employer to pay my wages into. It cannot be used for anything other than that. They are allowed to take any possessions that I have which are deemed to be luxuries. They allow you to keep essential items for living. My car is quite old and they let you keep a car up to a certain value. Mine comes within that criteria so I will be able to have a car to get me to work. Thankfully I have never been one for material possessions. As I have said before I am not a girly girl so I do not have expensive jewellery and once we looked into what the receivers can take from you there was not actually anything that we possessed that was worth taking.

The Court date has arrived and as Paul is not allowed to come with me he is going to wait in the car in the car park whilst I go in.

I find my way to the relevant floor and introduce myself to the court clerk. She points me to a seat and tells me to wait until I am called.

My legs are shaking so badly when they finally call my name that I am not sure I will be able to walk in. I am so terrified that as I walk through the door I fix my eyes on the Judge sitting waiting for me. I feel I need to focus on him or I am going to faint.

Once I am standing in the required position the Judge asks me to state my name and present address. He shuffles the papers in front of him and then begins to speak.

"I have read through your Statement and all the relevant documents and it seems to me that you have had rather a rough time of it." Tears begin to prick my eyes as this was something I had not expected. I nod, desperately trying to keep control of myself.

"Usually I would take a little longer than I am going to today. I must commend you for spending the past six months attempting to get on top of things. I am sure those companies that you managed to get paid off are very grateful for your efforts. I will not beat about the bush. I feel that you are well within your rights at this stage to request a Bankruptcy decision from the courts and I am therefore going to grant your request. Good luck for the future. The clerk will take it from here."

I was aghast, I did not even have to speak. He had literally just read the papers and made the decision. I managed to thank him and make my legs turn to leave as the court clerk came over to collect me. We barely made it out of the door before I burst into tears. I rather suspect the clerk was used to this sort of behaviour as she had tissues ready and she sat me down and went to fetch a glass of water.

Whilst I sat recovering the clerk explained that I would be contacted by the receiver's office who would need me to go to their offices in Southend-on-Sea. They would go through everything with me and it would be their responsibility to seize any goods that I had that they could sell at auction to help pay off the debts. They would also calculate what I would be able to live on per week and then the rest of my wages would be taken. This happens for a year and then my ties with the receivers will be over. The Bankruptcy ruling will however stay on my record for 5 years and in some cases forever.

I was then allowed to leave the court. As I walked out of the door and towards the car park to meet Paul I felt as though the weight of the World had been lifted from my shoulders. Two years had passed since we took on the pub, but now it was time to look forward, find myself a job and get on with our life.

One year later

What a difference a year makes.

I have been working for the Premier Inn as a receptionist. I managed to get the job very quickly after
becoming bankrupt and I love it. They are a great
team and I really enjoy the interaction with the guests. If
the housekeeping team are snowed under and we are quiet
on reception I will assist with the cleaning of the rooms.
Being able to just go to work and do my job without the
pressure of being in charge has been a delight. It has given
me time to lick my wounds and recover my broken mind.
Once I had established myself as a hard working member
of the team the Manager was happy to try and give me the
days off I asked for in order to get some days off with Paul.

At home Paul and I are always laughing and enjoying
our quieter life. We regularly talk about the pub and all
our adventures during that time. We also fully appreciate
the strength of our relationship. As Paul says, 'if we can
survive that time together, we can survive anything.' We
intend getting married one day, we just need to save up a
little first. The boys are all happy and settled and Rob is
loving his part of the house.

We are able to see more of Paul's sons now that we have more free time and that of course makes him very happy.

Jo and Richard took on a pub and are thoroughly enjoying it. They very sensibly rented out their house and took on a pub as Managers rather than Tenants which has given them a safety net that I had not considered; although maybe I am being hard on myself here as our circumstances were very different.

We regularly see Lyn, Dave and Luke. Lyn has been working with the new tenants and Dave and Luke still drink there. It is nice to catch up and hear how things are going. I confess we still have not been in for a drink. I feel it will be a long time before I can fight my demons and go back into the building that I miss so much.

Michael and Nick have moved into their own flat and I have taken Mikes' room and set it up as a reading room. Although I do not do many readings, it is a lovely space to just sit and relax, it has fabulous views out over the fields and it has a wonderful atmosphere in there.

I know that my guides are still with me, I regularly feel the presence of them all. Brian and Phoebe most especially when I am doing a reading. We have visited Glastonbury again and I think this will become an annual trip for us as we enjoy it so much and being able to climb the Tor and absorb some energy never ceases to thrill us.

Madeleine McCann has still not been found and my heart aches for her.

Today I have been asked by a friend if he can come and see me. He wants me to do my relaxation technique with him. I use my crystals when I do this. It is a mixture of crystal healing and a modification of the relaxation method I used when I gave birth to Michael and Christopher.

On arrival he tells me that he does not want a reading he just wants to be able to take a little time to completely relax. He has a stressful job and says he has been getting headaches and he thought that maybe I could help him.

The crystals are all laid out having been recharging in the sunlight.

"Just choose three of the crystals." I point him towards the table. "You will be guided to choose the right ones for you. I confess I do not even know what they are all meant to be good for. I have great faith in your guides pointing you in the right direction."

Once he has made his decision and he has his crystals I ask him to sit down.

I have a large reclining armchair in the room which is perfect for this type of session.

"Pull the lever to the side of the chair and then once the foot rest comes up push it with your feet until you are lying down. Once you are comfortable, place the three crystals on your skin. I would recommend one on your throat area, one midway down your chest and one on your tummy but I do want them on your skin not on top of your clothes."

I avert my eyes and busy myself with the CD player whilst he does this. When I am sure that he is comfortable and ready I ask him to close his eyes.

"I am going to talk you through the relaxation technique. Just allow yourself to become completely immersed in it. Do not be concerned if you feel you are falling asleep. When I finish speaking I will be putting on some music just to help you stay in your relaxed state. When it is time for you to come back I will talk you through it. Do not feel you have to suddenly be back with us, just take as much time as you like until you are ready to open your eyes. Is that all ok?"

He smiles and nods, eyes already closed and ready to begin.

I begin to talk. Keeping my voice low, calm and steady. I see his face begin to relax almost immediately and I know he will work well with this technique.

Once I have put the music on I sit back to relax. It feels a little odd. Usually during this time I allow the melody to wash over me and I open up to the spirit world, allowing them to come and begin the process of the reading but as he has said he does not want this I stare out of the window from where I am sitting in my armchair.

It occurs to me that he wanted this session as he is feeling stressed. Maybe I could ask the Angels for some healing. Almost the moment I think this, I am aware of an Angel entering the room. As with Brian he is very tall and he carries with him the most calming energy. I understand without having to ask that he has come to help me with the healing. I have been told in the past that I am a healer but it is one of those things that I find very hard to believe but I am always willing to try. As I close my eyes I concentrate on my friends head and from there I move my mind very slowly down the full length of his body. This probably only takes me a few minutes but by the time I reach his feet, I am feeling a strange mixture of tingling energy mixed with a slight tiredness.

I open my eyes and am aware that the Angel has gone from the room. When I look at the clock I am amazed to see that 15 minutes have passed since I began to play the music. Clearly I had been concentrating on the healing for longer than I had imagined.

I decide to give him a few more minutes whilst I try to get myself back on track. I close my eyes once more and allow myself to completely relax.

By the time I bring my friend out of his relaxation 'sleep' he has been in the room with me for 45 minutes.

"Wow," he said as he opened his eyes, "that was incredible." I think my surprise must have shown on my face because he clearly felt he should go on to explain.

"Whilst the music was playing I had the strangest feeling. I have been experiencing pain in my side for some time now. It is being investigated by the Doctor as they are not sure what it is. That whole area started to vibrate while I was relaxing. It felt like it got very hot too. But having said that, it did not stop me feeling utterly relaxed. I was aware it was happening but I was not concerned by it at all. If anything it was rather comforting."

I could feel myself gaping at him and he began to laugh.

"I guess you are not used to being told things like that."

"Well I admit that I felt a bit lost as you did not want a reading so I decided to attempt a little healing, although I was just thinking about easing your stress, it did not occur to me that anything else would occur but an Angel did turn up to assist."

"An Angel, I feel honoured." Now we were both looking shocked.

"Well let's hope we did some good between us." I said, still shaking my head in slight disbelief. Despite all I have been through with the spirit world it still manages to amaze me.

As I return to my room to blow out my candles after waving my friend goodbye I am deep in thought about what has just happened. Did I heal him with the assistance of an Angel? It is one of those questions that I will never really know the answer to. It still strikes me as incredible when I think about all the things that I have experienced but what I do know is that they bring me joy and that surely is the most important thing. I think I have learnt to just go with it and enjoy the ride.

As I walk into my room Phoebe is standing by the window. I jump as I was not expecting to see her there. She smiles at me, her adorable little face lights up as I enter the room.

She indicates my chair as if she wants me to sit down. I do as she asks and wait to see why she is here.

"I have come as I need to show you something." As she speaks I am shocked at how her voice sounds like that of an adult. At the same moment I realise that in all the time I have had her with me I have never heard her speak. She has always been at my side and given me extreme comfort but anything she has wanted to show me has been in the form of pictures. She has never actually spoken before.

"Since meeting Paul you have been through a period of 'Spiritual Awakening'. We knew that you were aware in some part of your abilities but until meeting Paul you had not completely embraced them. We also knew that you were about to enter a very turbulent time of your life and therefore I took the decision to make you aware of my presence at the start of this journey. You are a very maternal being and you have an affinity for young children. I therefore felt that this was the best way of joining with you, I knew you could accept my being with you to offer you comfort and support if I came to you appearing as I looked when I was a child.

Tears had begun to pour down my cheeks and I did nothing to stop them. I knew even before she said it what was coming and I was not sure I could cope with it.

"This will be hard Judith, you have come to love me as a child but I want you to know me as a Woman, for this is the way I prefer to be seen."

As she spoke she slowly began to transform, from my beautiful girl in her raggedy little dress, into a beautiful woman. She was dressed in a long dress which was rich in colour and suited her tall figure. She smiled gently at me and again began to speak.

"I will always be with you, I am one of your guides. I just wanted you to see me as I am. You will no longer see me as a child. You do not need that protection anymore."

I nodded through my tears and tried to smile but it was hard. I had very quickly learnt to love that little girl and this was really quite a shock. I understood what Phoebe was saying and slowly my mind began to accept how much this woman had helped me.

Finally I found my smile. "Thank you so much Phoebe, I know that you know how much you have helped me but I still want to say the words, thank you."

As she began to fade from view I knew that as she had said, she would always be with me.

"Never stop dancing my beautiful girl."

Acknowledgments

I have been reading books for as long as I can remember and when I look at the acknowledgments I am always touched by how many people are mentioned and just what is involved in writing a book.

This book, however, was reasonably easy for me as it is all true and so I did not have to do research or rely on the input of others.

But what I could not have done without, was the ever present support of all my family and friends. I am not going to start naming people as there are so many and they are all very important to me. But I do want to say thank you to each and every one of you. Your belief and encouragement never wavered and for that I am blessed.

I do of course just want to mention my darling husband Paul. How he managed to endure all of my tears and bouts of self-doubt I shall never know. But he did, he stood firm and continued to offer words of wisdom and faith in me and I shall be forever grateful.

I also want to thank Ujala Shahid who somehow managed to take the image out of my head for the book cover and make it into reality.

About the Author

Judith lives with her husband Paul in Maldon, Essex.

She has a passion for communication of any form. Judith very much enjoys public speaking and her guilty pleasure is social media on which, she admits, she spends far too much time.

People watching is a favourite pastime along with walking, socialising with friends and family, travelling with Paul, reading and playing with the Grandchildren.

Having dreamed for many years of one day writing a book; the opportunity finally presented itself during lockdown at the beginning of the 2020 pandemic.